GW00992010

MINDFUL
IS THE NEW
SKINNY

10

Transformational

Steps to a

Lighter You

Inside & Out

Jodi Baretz, LCSW, CHHC

Mindful Is the New Skinny: 10 Transformational Steps to a Lighter
You Inside & Out
© 2018 by Jodi Baretz, LCSW, CHHC

All rights reserved. Reproduction or translation of any part of this book through any means without permission of the copyright owner is unlawful, except for promotional use. Request for other permissions or further information should be addressed in writing to the author.

This book is not intended as a substitute for professional medical advice. The author/publisher shall have neither liability nor responsibility to anyone with respect to any loss or damage caused, or alleged to be caused, directly or indirectly by the information contained in this book. The reader should consult the appropriate healthcare professional regarding specific needs.

Client names in the case studies have been changed to protect their confidentiality.

ISBN-13: 978-1984157904
ISBN-10: 1984157906

Published by Kenco Press
Four Smith Avenue
Mount Kisco, NY 10549
www.jodibaretz.com

Editor: Gina Mazza (ginamazza.com)
Cover Design: Lynn McCormick
Interior Layout: Tamara Monosoff (tamaramonosoff.com)

Praise for
MINDFUL IS THE NEW SKINNY
and Jodi Baretz

At Integrative Nutrition, we believe that improving health and happiness can transform the world. This is exactly the message that Jodi espouses in this book. It's an informative guide to learning how to nourish yourself —not just with whole, healthy foods but, most importantly, a healthy attitude towards oneself and life. Jodi's perspective is fresh and lively yet profound.

— **Joshua Rosenthal, Founder and Director,
Institute for Integrative Nutrition, New York**

Jodi has done an incredible job writing a book that is accessible to all women striving to find peace, balance and contentment in their busy lives. I highly recommend learning from her personal story and following her practical and effective 10 steps.

— **Jeanette E. Cueva, MD, Associate Clinical Professor of Psychiatry, Columbia University College of Physicians and Surgeons**

We now have less attentiveness than a goldfish. This book has your answer to this dilemma.

— **Art DeLorenzo, Managing Principle,
Maximize Your Talent Group, LLC NYC, NY**

You may initially pick up this book to help yourself create a better relationship around food, but you will get so much more. Jodi provides a recipe for living your best life, broken down into relatable and actionable steps. She makes mindfulness doable. Give this book to every woman you know!

— **Ali Katz, author of *Hot Mess to Mindful Mom* and *Get the Most Out of Motherhood***

Upbeat, clear, completely user-friendly instructions for a mindfulness practice.

— Rachel Gerstein, PhD, Clinical Psychologist and
Mindfulness Practitioner

Wise and breezy, this guided journey shows how mindfulness can help us transcend stress and other negative elements that get in the way of our being our best in mind, body and spirit. Blending her trained expertise, real-life case studies and common sense, Jodi imparts invaluable insights and practical tools in an upbeat manner that is straight from the heart.

— Lisa D. Ellis, MS, RDN, CDN, LMSW, CEDRD

This book touches upon many of my triggers and feels like it was written for me. Brilliant.

— Isabel Simon, Literacy Expert

Jodi provides an easy-to-follow blueprint for helping you turn down the volume on negative thoughts, enhance your spiritual connection and get present so you can enjoy where you are in each moment.

— Michele Gregson, Westchester Women Chair,
UJA Federation, New York

Through playful yet reflective writing, Jodi provides an excellent and relatable approach for lasting happiness and a healthy self-image through the lens of mindfulness. This is THE guide for living a joyful, meaningful and authentic life free of self-judgment!

— Debbie Zeichner, LCSW, Parent Coach and Mindfulness
Educator

With clever insights, real-life case studies, accessible practices and just the right dose of science to back up her claims, Jodi makes a convincing case that mindfulness is the key to women finally being at peace with their bodies . . . and their lives.

— Laurie Simon-Kutcher, MS, RD, CDE

DEDICATION

*To my late father, Kenny Misher, who always encouraged me
to make my mark in this world; and my mother, Cookie Schwartz,
who taught me how.*

ACKNOWLEDGEMENTS

This book has been a long time coming and there are many people to thank for helping me bring it to fruition. Beverly West, thank you for starting me out on this journey by helping me organize my thoughts into chapters. It wasn't easy and took some time, but we made it through.

Deep gratitude to my clients, who inspire me and have trusted me to support them during their most vulnerable times. This book is for you. You are all so dear to me.

Special thanks to Breanne Zapien from Results VA, my virtual assistant and sounding board; and to Ali Katz for all the great tips and invaluable support. Thanks to Neil Gordon, who helped craft my "silver bullet" messaging.

Thanks to my amazing friends, who have always been super supportive and always encouraging. I am so lucky to have you! Dany, I am especially grateful for your morning phone call to check on my progress, and for your great feedback.

Thanks to Lauren Flick, who coached me through all my frustrations then took a lot off my plate towards the end when I needed it most. After all these years, I forgive you for losing my notebook in elementary school. You've more than made up for it!

Many thanks to my incredible editor, Gina Mazza, who made my words come alive and made me sound way more clever than I really am. I am truly grateful that I found her, as well as Tamara Monosoff whose guidance and support I couldn't do without.

I want to thank my amazing mother, Cookie, who gave me valuable feedback, encouraged me to keep going with her unrelenting pride, and was there for me through all the emergency calls and tough decisions. You are an inspiration and I love you! Eli, your support and meticulous last-minute editing was invaluable. I thank you. My two aunts, Isabel and Elyce gave me great feedback and cheered me to the finish line. My brother Ross, the licensing guru, I appreciate your feedback and I look forward to you making this a national brand. No pressure.

Thanks to Melanie, Andy and all my colleagues at The Center for Health and Healing for their tremendous support and for giving me the opportunity to practice what I am so very passionate about. It's a truly talented and special community.

I want to thank my sons, Alex and Brian, for inspiring me, teaching me and making me proud to be your mom every single day.

A special thank you to my husband, Lewis, who has given me time, space and coverage with the kids—not to mention helping with carpools and dinner—so that I could run my practice, go to trainings and write this book. As my friends often say, "Everyone needs a Lewis." I know it wasn't easy to put up with me at times, but I could never have done any of this without you and honestly couldn't have asked for a better life partner. One day, I know you'll meditate with me. No rush. I love you.

CONTENTS

INTRODUCTION

If you change the way you look at things,
the things you look at change.

— Wayne Dyer

Lisa came to my office for help because she struggles with her weight. She was tired of going on diets that she couldn't stick to and was increasingly frustrated. She knew what to eat and exercised regularly, but nothing seemed to work. After probing a little deeper into Lisa's life, she revealed many struggles and began to get teary. She shared that she was constantly stressed, overwhelmed and barely able to keep up with her many responsibilities. A wife and mother of two, Lisa found herself frequently short-tempered with her spouse and kids, typically turning to food to ease her frustrations.

This is a common scenario that many of us can relate to in our own lives. We are frustrated with the "restrictive dieting/overeating" rollercoaster. We beat ourselves up striving for perfection, rarely feeling "good enough." We not only struggle with our weight, but the stress and drama of daily life also weighs heavily on us. While we are laser focused on foods, diets and our bodies, we dismiss the real cause of our discontentment: our overactive stressed-out brains and hectic lifestyle. We are programmed to focus strictly on the body while neglecting the mind.

It's time to change our mindset, address our stress, and admit that something just isn't working. One of the major culprits is the fast-paced environment in which we live. Life moves so rapidly these days that we don't pay much attention to our thoughts and feelings or take care of our own needs. We are a generation of multi-taskers, with our attention constantly diverted from what we are doing in the moment. We rarely unplug from our smartphones, social media and Candy Crush, which are all designed to be addictive. In addition, we are constantly fed posts in our news feed of how "great" everyone else's lives are, which often makes us feel less than. To top it off, 24/7 breaking news creates ongoing anxiety and further distraction. As a result, the body ends up bearing the brunt of the stress we encounter. With all of this stimulation, it's no wonder we also have trouble sleeping.

I can personally relate to my client Lisa's story—in fact, her dilemma is partly why I choose to do the work that I do. As my children grew and I got older, with my many demands and a slowing metabolism, I couldn't get back to "skinny" no matter what I did. I was beyond tired of counting every calorie, not liking how I looked in my clothes, and berating myself in the process. What I didn't realize back then was that these overly self-critical thoughts affected my mood on a regular basis and sabotaged my weight loss efforts. What I know now is that I needed something completely different. *What I really needed was nourishment from the inside out.*

I'm not talking about nutrients in food—at least, not yet. I'm referring to the injustices that women, in particular, suffer from by constantly depriving themselves of not just food but self-compassion and self-care. There had to be another way, I reasoned, if only I could get out of my head, calm my cruel and self-degrading thoughts, and learn to be at peace with my "imperfect" self.

As I spoke with other women and learned from the clients coming in the door of my psychotherapy practice, it became clear that I wasn't alone. So many women are critical of their bodies and themselves, and the more I heard this from other women, the more it saddened me. I wanted to figure out a better approach to living for myself and others.

Looking back at my history with food, it has always been a complicated relationship, starting from when I was very young. I was a horribly picky eater and as a child my food groups were pizza and ice cream. As I got older, I was ordering off the kid's menu far longer than I should have been. Then in my thirties, I was diagnosed with Celiac Disease (an autoimmune condition wherein the body flags gluten as the enemy). This was an emotional and physical blow, but it turned out to be a blessing in disguise. I now had to be mindful of everything I put in my mouth.

My struggles with my new dietary restrictions gave me the inspiration to help others who face similar food intolerances and sensitivities. And so, at forty years old, I returned to school to become a health coach. It was an eye-opening experience that not only completely changed my eating habits but the quality of the food I was ingesting. I wasn't just cutting out gluten from my diet; I was changing my overall relationship with food. I also realized how powerful the mind-body connection is and that our emotional state has a huge impact on our bodies and our weight.

My school, The Institute for Integrative Nutrition, exposed me to other aspects of a holistic lifestyle—including spirituality, which I knew next to nothing about. This intrigued me because growing up as traditional and cultural Jew, I was never really exposed to spiritual teachings. My life-changing moment came when I was working with a mentor and she told me that there are so many things in life that we cannot control. Although it may seem obvious, it really stuck this time. Once we learn to loosen our grip and stop resisting what is, a freedom and lightness can come to us. This mentor was able to see life through a particular lens and I knew I needed to learn more.

After earning my certification in health coaching, I went on to study "Mindful Based Stress Reduction" (MBSR), which is a secular and scientifically based program. Like an absorbent sponge, I saturated myself in the topic of mindfulness—attending various retreats and seminars, as well as learning meditation and healing techniques. I am grateful to have joined the talented practitioners at The Center for Health and Healing in Mt. Kisco, New York, and to expand my private practice to include mindfulness-based psychotherapy and holistic health coaching. Integrating my professional offerings in this way has not only changed my life, but the lives of my clients.

I discovered something through this work that offers many solutions to the type of turmoil that Lisa, myself, and so many others go through every day. Mindfulness skills and concepts offer a different approach to eating, reducing stress and adopting a new attitude toward life. Learning to be with how things are in any given moment is transformational, and a skill worth developing.

The Mindful Is the New Skinny movement is based on the principle that if you nourish the inside, you will flourish on the outside. Once you drop the emotional weight and manage your stress better, only then will you look and feel your best.

I'm pleased to say that, as of this writing, Lisa is doing well. After she learned mindfulness concepts and techniques and discovered a new way to relate to her stress, her life significantly shifted. She resolved some long standing emotional issues that she never addressed in the past and were weighing her down. Her ability to tolerate her struggles (and cravings) improved, and she rarely reaches for food to comfort herself. Her newfound awareness allows her to listen to her body and its hunger cues so she never has to diet again. She is mindful about what she puts in her mouth but does not obsess, blame or punish herself for eating. She has healed her combative relationship with food; in fact, all of her relationships are better, especially with her kids. Though she is now happily two sizes smaller, her self-esteem is no longer tied to the numbers on her scale.

With the mindfulness techniques, concepts, case studies and short meditations contained within these pages, you will wake up to the inner workings of your mind, see how you create your own suffering and how the mind can be tamed. You will also learn how to shift your mindset from perfection and judgment to compassion for yourself, others and the daily struggles in your life. I've taken the time-honored concept of mindfulness and made it simple, clear, fun and relatable. My hope is that the mindfulness tools in this book enable you to find peace in your mind and your body.

HOW TO USE THIS BOOK

This book includes 10 steps to guide you toward a lighter you inside and out. Each step introduces a main concept, with personal anecdotes, case studies, mindful experiments and a short 10 minute meditation or two. Do one step at a time. I suggest you try one step a week and then return to the meditations any time you like.

This is an interactive book in which you can click a link or scan a QR code to listen to the meditations included. As a bonus for purchasing this book, with each step, you will get full access to a Meditation and Resource Library, where you will receive additional supplemental materials (such as recipes, shopping tips, articles, and more) to give you a full and complete mindful experience!

To use the QR codes in the print version: Hover over the codes with the camera on your phone, and it will open up to the meditations and resources. Otherwise, download a FREE QR code reader available in the APP store.

If you are reading an ebook, simply click on the links to access the meditations and resources.

PART ONE:

SELF-COMPASSION AND SELF-CARE

1

Enough Already! Taming Your Inner Critic

Hating your body won't make you thin, and being thin won't make you stop hating your body.

— Author Unknown

It's bright and early Saturday morning and I'm at the gym in yoga class, sporting my new breathable Athleta workout pants. I stake out my favorite spot in front of the mirror so I can check my alignment. The class begins peacefully in a lotus position on the mat. I inhale deeply and close my eyes. Ah yes, I'm so ready to let life's stresses fall away after a hectic week of responsibilities.

The instructor leads us into the first pose and I catch my look in the mirror. *Ugh. There's that darn muffin top flopping out of my waistband.* My head floods with thoughts of self-loathing. *Why can't I shrink my stomach? I eat healthy and exercise. It's not fair! The instructor is so skinny. I look so big next to her. Okay, stop obsessing and breathe. Cat and cow pose. This feels great on my back. Downward dog. Hold in those stomach muscles. That's better. Now into Warrior Two.*

I glance in the side mirror. *God, I hate my belly rolls. I'm not eating this week. I'm disgusting. Now I know why yoga studios don't use mirrors. Maybe I need to go to a studio instead of this gym. And on and on.*

So much for letting go of stress. Now I'm even more frazzled than when I walked into class.

Sound familiar?

Here's the upshot: None of the women in my class were noticing my muffin top because they were probably too busy obsessing about their own. For how accomplished, successful and "self-realized" we are as women, we're still plagued by criticisms about our physical appearance, particularly our weight, not just from the media and modern culture but from our own negative self-talk that we've internalized since forever. We are programmed to think that we need to look a certain way in order to be accepted, loved and, therefore, happy. It seems crazy, but it's reality.

Like it or not, most of us would probably admit that the saying, "You can never be too rich or too thin" holds a measure of truth. Case in point: one of my clients recently told me that she thinks being skinny equals power.

"Your life may be a shit show, but if you are skinny, you have it all," she shared.

How sad is that? Surely, other things in life matter more than what size jeans we fit into. If not, then I question how far we've truly come as females. What I'd like to suggest is that a great percentage of what's holding us women back from our *true* power stems not from society and culture, but our own inner monologue. If we can change that, we're off to a good start in achieving the self-acceptance and happiness that we falsely believe being skinny will bring us. Forget the number on the scale. You are not a wrestler, wearing your weight class on your sleeve. After all, what we are really going for is the feeling that being skinny offers us, not the number.

Lighten Up on the Fat Talk

Be honest. Have you become comfortable putting yourself down? Is accepting a compliment out of your comfort zone? Do you fixate on your imperfections instead of your assets?

Most of us struggle with being hard on ourselves, so if you've answered affirmative to the above questions, you're not alone. Psychologist and author Tara Brach, PhD calls it "the trance of unworthiness." We've all grown up in a society where competition is the norm. Perhaps your parents were your coaches in sports or other activities; or, at the very least, they tried to motivate you to be better in other ways such as academics, music or other talents. Sure, parents mean well and this can instill a great work ethic and encourage us to strive for success, but it can also leave a child feeling "not good enough." It's not just our parent's influence, of course. As humans, we seem to be made to always want more, be better and feel discontent with what we have and who we are; and social media has taken this to whole new level.

I'm not saying that life should always be a bowl of cherries (although they are a healthy snack). Disappointment and rejection happen in life, and we tend to subconsciously etch those experiences in our memories. No matter how many times our mothers may have told us that we're beautiful, the criticisms seem to stick the most. What we may not have known as children, we can embrace now: Beauty is an internal feeling, and what appears on the outside is an expression of that inner beauty.

Giving yourself a little self-love isn't selfish. In order to show compassion for others and love them well, you first need to show it to yourself. It's a two-way street: If we love and respect ourselves, others will do the same. If we are not kind and respectful to ourselves, how can we expect others to love and respect us, including our significant other? Having less-than-tight thighs or indulging in one too many desserts doesn't mean that you're an awful, unlovable person. Are you treating yourself as if you are?

Self-compassion is the new self-esteem. No matter what your current circumstance in life, self-compassion is invaluable even when self-esteem is low. This is a paradigm shift now becoming popularized, especially when it comes to parenting. A sense of false self-esteem (everyone gets a trophy) leads to entitlement, and if we can teach our kids how to be kind to themselves from an early age, they will be a lot better off. But first we have to do this for ourselves. So, lighten up on the servings of fat talk and add in a main course of self-compassion. In fact, eliminate self-judgment from your daily mind-diet altogether.

You might be thinking that this is easier said than done. The first step is awareness. Notice and listen to the words that come out of your mouth or pass through your mind. Would you think about or speak the same way to your best friend, or even someone who you don't particularly care for? If not, then why would you talk that way to yourself?

When negative thoughts pop up, as they undoubtedly will, first be aware of them. Acknowledge the thought then let it go, giving it no further attention. Know that these thoughts are just recurring out of habit. That is the nature of the mind. Don't berate yourself for it. Just become aware then press "stop" on the tape as often as you need.

Next, refocus on something good about yourself. You have many amazing qualities but do you notice and appreciate them? One of my clients was constantly belittling herself for her weight, so I asked her to make a list of things she loved about herself. She was extremely uncomfortable with this exercise but she did it. (If this exercise is difficult for you, as well, then you really need to do it!) This simple process helped shift her self-view from her weight to her many admirable qualities, including being a great partner and being brilliant in her career.

The rewards for making this mind shift are worth it. Once you get a handle on how you speak to yourself, you will notice a great many changes. Not only will it help you stay away from self-destructive binges, you will move forward in virtually every aspect of your life—from productivity to more harmonious relationships to experiencing more joy and peace. An amazing freedom comes from not worrying about what everyone else thinks. It only really matters what you think, and you can "change your mind." I have a good friend who once told me, "Well, I think I look cute, so who cares what everyone else thinks." She is my idol. It's refreshing. She simply values her own opinion over everyone else's. I'm not suggesting you feed yourself BS. What I'm saying is that focusing on your positive qualities and feeling good about yourself will have a positive effect on your attitude and confidence. You will feel worthy and capable. You need to feel good to look good. Just try it and see what happens.

• • •

The following client case study illustrates how self-sabotage was affecting her weight, relationships and life in general—until she was able to shift her self-talk.

CASE STUDY:
The Perfectionist Binge Eater

Kelly, a single mom who lives with her fiancé, came to me wanting to lose 20 pounds that she'd gained over the previous year. She was training for a marathon and wanted to get back to her "fighting" weight and eat properly. Kelly has an extremely competitive personality, especially when it comes to herself. Her main issue with her nutrition is that she has constant cravings and occasionally binge eats.

When I first met Kelly, one of the things I noticed immediately is how she speaks to herself. She degrades herself and almost constantly compares herself to others. A perfectionist, Kelly beats herself up for any behavior that she perceives as less than perfect. She shared with me that her mother was tough on her while growing up, always criticizing her. Kelly could never be thin enough, pretty enough or smart enough—which left her feeling inadequate. Ironically (or not), when Kelly's mother passed away, she chose to get plastic surgery with the inheritance money.

"It's what my mother would have wanted," she said.

Kelly's behavior was causing tension in her relationship with her fiancé. She was not able to accept his loving feelings at times and would push him away. As we dug deeper into the root cause of this, Kelly admitted that she felt undeserving of his admiration, even doubting the sincerity of the compliments he gave her.

Not knowing what to do, Kelly turned to food to soothe her

feelings of inadequacy and shame. Most of our work together centered on reversing the years of self-talk based on her mother's disapproval. Gradually, her self-perception began to shift. She was able to separate out her mother's opinions—which were based on her experiences and biases—from her own.

Kelly rediscovered what she liked about herself, including that she is a great athlete, an amazing mom and a hard worker. She could also appreciate that she has beautiful eyes and a great laugh. Once Kelly was able to see her strengths, accept her imperfections and, ultimately, change her self-talk, those 20 pounds melted off because she no longer binged out of self-loathing. Her relationships also improved as a result. These days, Kelly graciously accepts compliments from her soon-to-be-hubby and feels worthy of his love. She's going to be a glowing bride!

MINDFUL EXPERIMENT:
Mind Over Fatter

The following experiment will help you correct the less-than-desirable self-talk. (I like to use the word experiment because you can "test" what works for you.) As I mentioned earlier, the first step in disrupting your inner monologue is to become aware of it. Only then can you change it.

1. For at least one week, pay attention to and how you talk to and about yourself. What you are saying and how often are you repeating it? Make a list and study it. Do you see any patterns? Where do you think these beliefs come from?

2. Now rewrite the list, replacing those negative statements with positive ones. If you feel uncomfortable doing this, just notice how it feels to say loving things to yourself. What are your best characteristics? Do you like your eyes, legs, hair? What about personality traits; are you quick witted, caring or generous? Are you a loyal friend or hard worker? Focus on what you love about yourself and be grateful for it.

3. Come up with your own affirmation or use this one: "Even though I am not perfect, I am strong, smart and beautiful as I am."

4. Begin to notice when you are in a negative story about yourself; interrupt the story and refocus on the task at hand. It's usually helpful to name this narrative, such as the "I'm not good enough" story. This makes your self-talk fictionalized and separate from you.

5. After weeks of doing this experiment, notice how others change around you. Play with this and have fun watching others' responses to your new attitude.

Mindfulness: The Ultimate Mental Cleanse

How many times have you missed an exit while driving or not really paid attention when someone was talking because your mind was not focused on what you were doing? Being on autopilot can be useful at times because we don't have to relearn things, but it also contributes to us missing many of the moments of our lives because we are "somewhere else."

Mindful simply means aware, but let's take a moment to define "mindfulness." According to world-renowned mindfulness expert Jon Kabat-Zinn, PhD, mindfulness is an awareness that arises when you pay attention to the present moment in a particular way without judgment. Although it is a mouthful, it is really quite simple. It is observing what is happening in the moment without resisting it, allowing things to be as they are. Your mind is focused on the present, not pushing away your current experience or thoughts and feelings, positive or negative.

Mindfulness is acknowledging what is happening and accepting that you cannot control outer circumstances like the weather or your child having a tantrum at Target (most moms have been there). With this awareness, you can choose to respond skillfully and gracefully to a broad range of emotions and become less reactive. In short, it is moment-to-moment compassionate awareness.

It doesn't matter what dogma you follow or belief system you may have; anyone can learn to be mindful and tame the inner critic by paying full attention to what is happening right now. Even if you don't like what is happening with your body or your current life situation, focusing on the present moment is much healthier and productive than being lost in past or future thoughts. We can't change things if we are not aware of what is happening and its impact on us. True, we tend to resist what we don't like or can't control, but the situation is what it is, so you may as well feel it, allow it to be there, and learn something from it. This doesn't mean we don't change what we can; in fact, we can do both; acknowledge the reality and then act.

The point is, we have a choice in terms of our attention, so we may as well pay attention to the thoughts that serve us and let the negative ones pass right on by. Still, we can't help how we feel, so not pushing feelings away can help us process and release them. We are judgmental creatures with opinions about everything, wanting control. Letting go and going with the flow can be liberating. The same logic applies to you. Not judging where you are in your life and with your body is crucial. There are reasons why you are where you are, and the inner critic doesn't help. So, drop the destructive commentary and move through any resistance, being patient and kind with yourself. Just remember that you may not have the full picture as to why things happen. Inherent in some of the most challenging times are life's greatest lessons—and that's not just a cliché.

The Five A's of Mindfulness:

ATTITUDE. Cultivate a compassionate attitude toward daily life.

AWARENESS. Become aware of your thoughts and feelings.

ATTENTION. Focus on what is happening right now.

ACCEPTANCE. Have an open mind about what is happening in the moment, without resistance.

ACTION. Now that you are calm, take action, as needed. Remember that mindfulness is not passive. Take appropriate action but accept what you cannot change.

Meditation: A Mental Gymnasium

Meditation is the exercise that you do to become more mindful. There are many stereotypes about meditation (that are slowing going away as it becomes more mainstream). If you still consider it a bit "woo-woo", it might help to think of it simply as a 'brain training exercise.' Just like we work out our bodies at the gym, meditation is "personal training" for the mind. And just as our muscles may ache from physical exercise at the start of a workout program, we may also resist meditation until we have built our "mindfulness muscles." Now, many of you may be thinking, *I could never meditate because my mind is always "on" and I can't quiet it down.* Guess what? You are the ones who need it the most (and FYI, we all have minds that are always on). That's like saying, "I'm so out of shape, I could never exercise." So, let's just get over that. I am not asking you to stop thinking (that's impossible); rather, I'm suggesting that you change your relationship to your thoughts by not getting caught up in them and bringing your attention back to your breath. It's simple, really. Breathe, think, breathe, think… over and over. It may help to picture in your mind that you are in an egg spoon race and you have to pay attention to the egg while you're moving to prevent it from breaking. Your thoughts are moving fast but you are focused on the egg.

Why should you meditate? That's a no brainer (pun intended). It is the best way to settle your overactive mind and redirect yourself to the present moment. It is your mind that creates your discontentment, so learning to master it creates more inner peace. Think of shaking up a snow globe. Your thoughts are the snow going crazy inside of it. When you simply let it sit, what happens? It settles, and eventually so will your mind. Meditation also has a ton of added benefits for your emotional and physical health. Stress reduction is a big one, along with improved focus, productivity and empathy. Reducing stress has been shown—big bonus (wait for it!)—to be very effective for weight loss as well.

Now that you know what meditation is and why it's good for you, let's step through how to begin a simple formal practice.

- If possible, meditate around the same time every day; for example, first thing upon waking or before you go to sleep. See what works for you.

- Choose a comfortable place to meditate on a regular basis. It can be on a chair, couch or cushion in a quiet corner of your living space. If you are sitting on a cushion, make sure your knees are lower than your hips to support your back.

- Sit in a dignified and alert posture that is not conducive to sleep. I like to say, "upright but not uptight." Be comfortable, but no slouching.

- Put your hands gently on your knees, palms up or down, and pull them slightly back to open your chest.

- Again, the goal is not to block out thoughts but to change your relationship to them. When your mind wanders, simply come back to your breath.

- When you're ready, close your eyes and take a few deep breaths. Start by following the guided instructions in the meditation videos (see QR code links) at the end of each chapter. Once you get the hang of it, you can meditate on your own.

- Bear in mind that this is a practice. It takes time to get used to but is so worth it, I promise.

. . .

So, now let's stop talking about meditation and actually give it a whirl! Below are two meditations that will get your practice started, accompanied by "Mindful Mantras"— my take on short, simple yet powerful affirmations that I'd like you to lightly keep in the back of your mind as you go about your day. Everything else you need to know is contained in the meditation. Ready? Scan the link then allow me to guide you by listening to the meditation online.

LET'S MEDITATE:

BUT, I CAN'T MEDITATE! SHOW ME HOW

This "general awareness of breath" meditation can be practiced on a daily basis.

Listen to the meditation here:

http://www.mindfulisthenewskinny.com

MINDFUL MANTRA:

I can meditate.
I just need to practice and give myself the chance.

LET'S MEDITATE:

I'M BEATING MYSELF UP. MAKE ME STOP!

This meditation will help you quell critical thoughts and practice self-compassion.

Listen to the meditation here:

http://www.mindfulisthenewskinny.com

MINDFUL MANTRA:

I may not be perfect but I am strong, smart and beautiful just as I am.

MINDFUL MEMO:

- Stop wasting your mental energy on hating your body. Love and accept yourself without judgment and destructive self-talk.

- You are your own best friend, so act like it and be kind to yourself.

- Treat yourself like you would someone you love, like a child or a pet. Teach people how to treat you. Accept where you are right now in order to move forward.

- Notice when you are in a negative "story" and redirect your mind to the present moment.

- Meditate on a regular basis to silence your inner critic and redirect unwanted thoughts.

2

You're Grounded!
Finding Your Center

I realized that I don't have to be perfect. All I have to do is show up and enjoy the messy, imperfect and beautiful journey of my life.

—Kerry Washington, Actor

If you associate the phrase "getting grounded" with punishment as a kid for staying out too late with your friends, and "finding your center" to mean where the nearest shopping mall is located, we've got some work to do.

All kidding aside, what I'm about to propose as the second step in your mindfulness journey is serious business, because it can truly help you "lighten up." Getting grounded, in our context here, refers to being mentally and emotionally stable. Merriam Webster adds that it can also mean "admirably sensible, realistic and unpretentious." Mental and emotional stability is a commodity these days due to the countless demands placed on us—and that we place on ourselves, consciously and unconsciously. (Seriously, how many times do you check your smartphone in a day? An hour?) At my nutrition school, we were taught that "primary food" (your relationships, career, what feeds your soul) is more important than what you put on your plate. As women, we tend to put everyone else's needs first. We take on too many tasks and strive to be perfect in all of them, like a modern-day Wonder Woman. We're not always "sensible and realistic" when it comes to cramming in our "to do" lists for the day.

So, you may wonder what a woman is to do about this. At times, it means digging those Christian Louboutin heels into the ground and saying "no" to taking on too much. This is an essential skill for a balanced, authentic and meaningful life, in addition to setting boundaries. Women tend to say "yes" to what others want at the expense of themselves; we never want to disappoint. Parents may not approve of the choices we make. Friends may not like that we can't watch their dog for the weekend or go out for a girl's night. Getting push-back from others and always doing what others want and expect can wear you down. Saying "yes" when you really mean "no" can have a dangerous effect on your self-worth, esteem and waistline.

I once had a friend who would constantly ask me to go out and do things with her. This was great until I realized that I did not want to do half of those things. I did them out of guilt and fear of disappointing her. Eventually, I wo-manned up and learned to decline the invites that did not work for me. While this did affect the friendship by throwing it off balance, I became a whole lot happier. I am not the type who needs to be busy all the time. That was how she functioned, not me. I enjoy the peace and comfort of my own home. Women also tend to do things that we feel we "should" be doing for outward appearances. For example, one friend once told me that she was done going to museums. She never liked them but thought she "should" go. Once she stopped, her vacations became a lot more fun and adventurous, which was more her speed.

Put Yourself First, For Once

I get it. Women are the managers and caretakers—of our kids, our aging parents and extended families, even our spouses, and, of course, our homes. If you are an entrepreneur or in a management-level position in a company, you've got the added responsibility of leading your team. So, what does the flight attendant say when preparing the cabin for liftoff? You've heard it before yet it bears repeating: Put the oxygen mask on yourself before assisting anyone else, including loved ones. If you're gagging for air in your life because you're stretched so thin, there's no way you're going to be able to help anyone else.

I'd like to give a quick shout-out to all the moms out there because being a parent is its own juggling act. Parenting is mostly joy, but not always fun. Nobody really tells you how isolating, physically exhausting and downright miserable it can be at times. It truly is an endurance test but it shouldn't be a display of martyrdom. Life should go on… for YOU, I mean. Every once in a while, get over the guilt and get a freakin' babysitter. When you are with your children, incorporate your practice of being present so your time together is focused on quality and not quantity. It's more beneficial to your kids if you put down the phone and the laundry and give them your full attention for half an hour than to be with them 24/7, chronically screaming while you're trying to get 20 other things done simultaneously. It is true that children grow up in the blink of an eye, so cherish your time, knowing that you will once again be able to refocus on your own goals and desires in life down the road, and the laundry will get done eventually, too!

Let's go back to the Wonder Woman analogy for a moment. When you *are* tending to your family, I recommend that you drop the fantasy of everything being perfect. Do not fantasize about impersonating the feisty, fun-loving bombshell Gloria from "Modern Family" who walks around the house all day in heels and slinky dresses—come on, even Sophia Vergara doesn't do that. (I do, however, recommend getting out of your sweatpants once in awhile). Listen, I understand how many mini medicine balls you are juggling. Many of us take care of our homes, have a career, raise the kids, cook the meals, and act as our family's social director and much more, in addition to trying to maintain our appearance and have a fit bod. It can be overwhelming. Again, it comes back to taking time to pamper yourself a bit without feeling selfish. Yes, you want to achieve your goals on all fronts in life and you want to be flawless while doing so, but don't get caught up in that never-ending cycle of stress and striving. Use your growing practice of presence to help you determine what's truly important and what isn't going to matter in the long run.

CASE STUDY:
CEO Mom

Abby is a working mom of two, ages 15 and 12. She came to me because, as she reports, her "brain has no off switch." She works long hours, has a demanding job and family, and never seems to stop going. She works all day, does more work while on the train commute home, and jumps right into family mode when she gets there. Even when Abby has some free time, she doesn't know what to do with it, and tries to complete her "to do" list, which is always a running commentary in her head. She is aware that this is no way to live and wants to do something about it but cannot change her responsibilities.

Abby is a great leader at work and has several associates that she manages. I told her to think of her mind as the associates that are always trying to interrupt her, and that she is now the CEO of her mind. At first, she couldn't change her thoughts but eventually whenever the "to do" voice came in, she changed her response: She would thank the thought for warning her but that it would have to wait until she was ready to "take the meeting" and address its needs. I instructed her to not give the commentary any attention until that "later date" and only focus on the task at hand.

I have no doubt that this strategy of "organizing her mind" will make Abby a better leader at work. We could not resolve the amount of responsibilities she has, but did address how all the energy she spends thinking about what she has to do in the future is draining her. Giving herself permission to not always be "doing" gave her a huge sense of relief. She can't be everything to everyone and will sometimes have to miss activities or events to do other things she needs to accomplish, but when she does *anything*, the goal is for her to be fully present. Abby also had to learn to let go of some control and delegate some responsibilities at work and at home, too, even if things weren't done exactly as she would do them.

We agreed that she would start training her brain while on her

2 - You're Grounded! Finding Your Center

commute to and from work. She agreed to work on the train only until she was 20 minutes away from home. Then she would switch to listening to a meditation for 10 minutes, then sit in silence for the last 10. In these moments, Abby simply stayed present. She looked at the scenery along the route, felt her body in the chair, smelled the surrounding scents, and listened to whatever sounds were in her environment. Doing so made her feel grounded and centered before she reached home, and like a palate cleanser, she was refreshed for the next course of her day: family time. She came to learn that she could slow down time by meditating for only 10 minutes. (It's like gaining an extra hour, a bonus daylight savings time!)

Abby immediately felt better upon putting these simple practices in place. She is relieved that she didn't have to give up anything, just change the way she relates to her tasks. She now replaces multi-tasking and multi-thinking with focusing on one thing at a time. She now has more energy and is more productive in her days—and yes, she is now the CEO of her own mind.

Ease the Burden

Beyond being mindful, what else can you proactively do to bring more balance and ease into your life? Here are a few big ones:

Delegate responsibilities to others. Most of us ladies don't let others help us because how others do something might be "wrong" or not as good as we would do it. (Sometimes, we're right about that!) We often think it's easier to just do everything ourselves.

What would happen if you let go? When my kids were born, my husband tended to be a bit controlling when it came to the kids. Whenever I would step in to do something when he was around, he would inevitably take over. Granted, he is a worker bee, and I am way more laid back. At first, I was offended by his help and struggled for control. Then I realized that even if things were not done as I would do them, they still got done. The world didn't end. I'm not going to lie to you, once I got over the "my way or highway" attitude, I milked this for a while, letting him shoulder the responsibilities; but it was definitely stressing him out. To his credit, he is learning to give up some control.

Even though you may be in the opposite situation, let's consider for a moment how we make others feel when we are control freaks. Many husbands don't take equal responsibility with caring for the children or the household. Let's be mindful and consider why. Could they possibly feel like if they take the initiative, they will never meet our expectations? Do you tend to jump in every time he tries to help? When we are hypercritical of others, as my husband was at times, it makes the other person want to give up. Bring awareness to your own actions and take responsibility, when needed.

Speak up when necessary. Delegating to others and keeping yourself on the priority list along with everyone else simply won't happen if you don't communicate your needs. Don't assume that anyone— including those who love you the most—know what you want.

One woman I recently worked with blamed her husband of 30 years for her unhappiness. She didn't realize it but one of her underlying resentments was that she was tired of cooking dinner for him night after night. This was her role and felt it was expected of her, but their kids were grown and she'd had enough. Just because this was their way of life didn't mean it had to continue. So she brought this up to him. Initially, he resisted, but she stood strong and eventually he came around to the idea, even bringing home take-out meals. It was only after she spoke up that he realized how unhappy she was and offered to help. This was a big relief to her and some of her resentment dissipated. It can be an adjustment to change a long-term dynamic but with communication and boundaries, change can happen.

Again, your mindfulness practice will help you to communicate your needs more effectively because it will cause you to slow down and ask yourself what you really need in any given moment. If you don't know what you want or need, well, that's just going to confuse everyone. So, it's your responsibility to pay attention, stay centered and use a level head when making decisions and determinations.

Know what you want. Right about now you may be thinking, *what if I don't know what I want?* Aside from diamonds, a vacation to Cabo and this season's Tory Burch handbag, it can be challenging to know not only what we want but how to make decisions around our own "buy in." Choices have consequences, so how do you know that you are making the right ones?

As women, we can be indecisive and over-analytical. This is where calming the mind and listening to your inner wisdom comes in handy. Listen to the wisdom of your body as well. See how it feels physically when you decide one way or another. Use your "gut brain" by noticing sensations in your body that will tell you if something doesn't feel right. Maybe you will notice a tinge in your stomach or heaviness in your heart. Do your muscles tense up or relax? Your intuition knows the answer before your brain does. Your mind gets in its own way but your gut is pure wisdom.

Here's a lighthearted coin trick you can use to tune into your body's response and help you make a decision. Assign heads or tails to either choice, and make sure you promise yourself that you will stick with the outcome. Toss a coin and whatever comes up, follow it. Immediately after the toss, pay attention to your body. How do you feel? You will know right away if this is truly what you want. Did your stomach drop? Did you feel excited, relieved or regretful? Did your body tense? Pay attention and your body will give you the answer.

Lose the clutter. Clutter makes us feel like our lives are as disorganized as a three-ring circus and that our jobs are never done. But as you become more mindful, minimalism becomes more important than materialism. Less is more, which simplifies our lives since there is less to maintain. Remember Abby from our earlier case study? Just moving piles of paper from her kitchen to her office made her less anxious when she walked in the door.

Our closets are a good example of how we subtly add stress to our environment and our lives. We typically wear 20 percent of the clothes 80 percent of the time. All the extra clothes make it harder to get dressed in the morning and take up precious space. I had a friend that wanted to move because her house was too small, but after she packed up, tossed a bunch of stuff and saw all the space she actually had, she questioned her decision. If you are attached to your stuff and afraid to get rid of it, try packing up boxes of things you think you may regret giving away, so it's out of sight for a period of time. If you don't end up looking for it, toss it for good.

MINDFUL EXPERIMENT:
From "To Do"
to "Ta Da"

- Take a moment to notice what tasks you do during the day and write them down. Pay attention to how they make you feel and if they are truly essential. Ask: Does this task bring me joy? Is there another way to accomplish this? What can I farm out? Do I engage in too many time-wasters like social media?

- Prioritize the most important tasks that need to be done this week. Make another list of things to be accomplished in the next month or so. Go to your calendar and schedule times when you can attend to these tasks—first weekly then monthly. Be careful not to overbook yourself. Reserve some space for self-care and things that come up unexpectedly.

- Now make another list of five enjoyable things that want to do for yourself. (It can't be doing something for your kids.) Some examples would be spending more time with friends, having quiet creative time, savoring a good novel, just having downtime, or even getting more sleep. The key is to start with one thing and make time for it, even at the expense of the other items on your "to do" list. Carve out the space then add it in to your calendar. When you have that one in your routine, move down the list and add another one in, and so on.

- Notice when you say "yes" to things that you don't want to be doing. Practice saying "no" in those situations. How do others react? Is the house of cards still standing? Are you living the life you want to live or living based on others' expectations? Get off the hamster wheel and stop doing things that don't work.

- De-clutter one area of your house and pack stuff away, but don't get rid of the box just yet. See if you actually reach back into it. If not, sell it, donate to a good cause that could use it, or throw it away.

I'm Not for Everybody

People will love you and people will hate you. And none of it will have anything to do with you.

— Abraham Hicks

I often quip, "I'm not for everybody." My husband reminds me of this from time to time when others are not enchanted with me. I tend to be very direct; at times, this is an asset and in other instances it doesn't win me any friends. I laugh about it now, but it took me awhile to get comfortable with the fact that not everybody approves of my actions, agrees with the things I say, appreciates the work I do, or even likes me. That's okay. I can respectfully agree to disagree with someone. A person unsubscribing from my newsletter, for example, is not an affront to my very being. Keeping things in the proper perspective is healthy and wise.

Yet it's not always easy peasy. We are hard wired to detect the "negative" for our very survival. The part of our brain called the amygdala is responsible for detecting fear and other emotions, and preparing us for emergency situations. We have to find a way around the reflexive negative thinking that ultimately leads to self-doubt, stress and extra pounds. Meditation, learning how to pause before reacting, and remembering not to personalize everything are all important in helping to accomplish this.

I got a powerful chance to practice this when someone in my town wrote in a national blog about my mindfulness group in an unfavorable light, without having met me, attending my group, or knowing anything about my practice. She basically spun an article that I wrote to serve her purposes, even taking quotes by me and others out of context. At first, I was shaken by the sheer audacity of what she did, but then I felt flattered that my work was important enough for her to notice and take time to respond to. I could see, through the lens of not taking her comments to heart, that her criticism—while written "about" me—really had nothing to do with me. I let things play out and the end result actually benefitted me, as I was given more name recognition in this locale, which led to bringing even more clients onboard. Had I responded with an angry backlash, that probably wouldn't have been the case. See how "pausing" can be beneficial.

As humans, we all want to belong, which is how we survive, physically and emotionally. If we stay authentically ourselves, we will belong to the groups where we are meant to belong; however, if we strive to "fit in", this means we are changing ourselves to please others, which is not allowing ourselves the freedom to be our true selves. Similar, but so different. Make sense?

Why is it so important to us what others think of us? This originally comes from wanting to please our parents. As kids, when we weren't testing limits or driving them bat shit crazy, we wanted their approval and love. Then this expanded into wanting our peers to like us. The crazy stuff we did as teens to fit in was epic, if not extraordinary. The peer group becomes everything. From an evolutionary perspective, if we got kicked out of the tribe (peer or family unit), we would most likely die. This is why we are conditioned to fit in, want others to like us, and be a part of the group. Again, belonging is important, but fitting in is not.

What others think of us is never usually about us anyway. It is just their opinion, and if we let it get to us, it can damage our progress and self-worth. It's usually about them and what pushes their buttons, based on their past experiences. That's why some will be drawn to you and others not so much, even if you are the same person to all. Don't let others get in your head and derail your awesomeness. (Read more about this in the book *The Four Agreements* by Don Miguel Ruiz.)

We also need to realize that others rarely treat us differently than they would anyone else in their lives. It really isn't personal. Just pay attention to their behaviors in other situations and you will see what I mean.

I had a friend whom I'll call Shari, who would always make me feel like crap about myself whenever she didn't get her way. She had many friends but I always thought that she only "bullied" me. One day, I ran into another friend of hers and asked if she ever felt that Shari treated her like she treated me. To my surprise, she said that everything I felt, she felt. This was a big relief and an eye-opening conversation. To my surprise, I discovered many other mutual friends who felt the same way. If you ever believe that someone in your life does something just to you, look around because it's probably their modus operandi with everyone. Take some time to notice this next time someone disappoints you or treats you a certain way.

CASE STUDY:
The Codependent Eater

Taking things personally can absolutely affect the way we eat and, as a result, impact our health. This was the case with Jill, a married woman with two teenage boys. She wanted to work with me because she was unhappy with her body and wanted to lose weight. Jill often compared herself to her thin friends and felt inadequate around them. Jill had reached a point where she couldn't tolerate being in her body anymore, and her husband, Jason, often pointed out her extra weight in a derogatory way. He was emotionally abusive at times and would often call her "fat." This made her turn to food for comfort, hence perpetuating the vicious cycle.

I began to work with Jill on accepting herself and her body. She would make good strides then Jason would push her emotional buttons and derail her progress. Then one day in a session, we discovered that Jill's husband was actually unhappy with himself, not her, and was borderline depressed. Further digging into Jason's upbringing revealed that he was constantly berated by his family; thus, this was all he knew how to do. In fact, for him, in a distorted kind of way, it was his means of showing love.

Once Jill unwound Jason's issues from her own, she learned to not personalize what he was saying to and about her. I recommended that she become aware when he was having one of his negative rants and not assign it any personal meaning. We referred to this as Jason's "Unhappy with Myself" story, and she didn't get caught up in it.

As difficult as it was, Jill became good at identifying when Jason was going off on her based on his own issues, and learned to not personalize his anger. As Jill changed, her husband took notice. It made him take a close look at himself and he was able to eventually be more aware of what he was doing (especially since he was now fighting alone). This inspired Jason to seek counseling for himself as well.

Once Jill broke this cycle of codependency with her spouse and let go of her inner (and outer) dialogue of unworthiness, she was able to nourish herself and not overeat, which led to the weight loss she desired.

Not Too Loose, Not Too Tight

[Once] the Buddha asked a musician how he tuned his instrument before playing. The musician said, "If I tune the strings too tight, they break. If I tune them too loose, no sound will come out. So not too tight and not too loose works best." To which the Buddha replied, "This is how you should hold your mind in meditation."

As you can see, it's crucial to not let other people's criticisms or actions blow you around like the wind. We can't control anyone else's behavior. Of course, people and external events will bring us joy or sorrow, but the key is to not be thrown off center, thereby reaching for a hunk of layer cake to soothe you. I am referring to the concept of equanimity, or staying calm in the midst of chaos. Balance is all about not holding on too tightly one way or the other.

LET'S MEDITATE:

IT'S ALL TOO MUCH! I NEED CALM IN THE CHAOS

This meditation (adapted from Jon Kabat-Zinn's mountain meditation in his MBSR program) will help you become strong and stable so you can execute your responsibilities well and not let the judgments and actions of others affect you.

Listen to the meditation here:

http://www.mindfulisthenewskinny.com

MINDFUL MANTRA:

No matter what comes my way,
I handle it with grace and ease.

MINDFUL MEMO:

- Taking care of yourself and putting your needs first will make you a better caretaker in the long run, in addition to making you the best you can be.

- Don't be Wonder Woman. Perfection is not possible.

- It's okay to say "no" sometimes and set boundaries. "No" is a complete sentence.

- Remember that you are not going to be able to please everyone.

- You can't control others' behaviors; you can only control your own.

- Don't allow your thoughts or others' criticisms or actions throw you off balance and drive you to overreactions.

PART TWO:

HEALTHY AND MINDFUL EATING

3

Ditch the Die-It Mindset. It Doesn't Work!

By choosing healthy over skinny, you are choosing self-love over self-judgment.

— Dr. Steve Maraboli

I'm going to lose weight even if it kills me.

Have you found yourself saying this, even if you don't mean it literally? Or have you ever wished for a nasty stomach bug so you could shed a few pounds? It's time for a new attitude toward food and your body, and it's not about following a die-it.

First things first: The diet must die.

Consider these sobering facts: If diets worked, we would be a nation of thin people. At any given moment, there are about 24,000 diet programs on the market and around 20 million people attempting to lose weight. Yet UCLA researchers who conducted a rigorous analysis of 31 long-term diet studies concluded that one may lose weight on a diet initially, but most gain back the weight, plus more. A minority of participants in the UCLA-based research sustained their weight loss, while a majority completely regained their weight and probably would have been better off not going on a diet at all! There you have it. Diets are unsustainable and are usually a vicious cycle of restriction and overeating. On and off. Good and bad. All or none. We cannot sustain long-term restriction so our willpower wanes, we fall off the chuck wagon and start to overeat again—the next time with gravy added.

But let's back that wagon up for a minute. We seem to have given into the societal norm of valuing ourselves based on our weight to the point where we'll do anything to thin down. What's with that? Many women who are unhappy with their bodies desperately try to lose those extra pounds and when they reappear, they are angry—mostly with themselves. They may feel like it's their fault.

Guess what? It is most likely *not* their fault. The body is a complex machine and many factors may contribute to weight gain or loss. Genetics, hormones, metabolism, medications, sleep, stress, and the body's natural set point are a few, so let's review these.

Genetics give us certain body types and it is not easy to fight the power of DNA. Some are luckier than others in this area, but the naturally thin girls would starve in a famine (if that's any consolation). As the UCLA research indicates, each time you lose and gain, it's harder to lose weight the next time. Why? Yo-yo dieting wreaks havoc on your metabolism and with each diet you lose muscle as well.

Hormones and medications can also affect our ability to lose that stubborn weight. Our bodies have a natural set point, a homeostasis, of where it wants to be, so if you go way below it, the body will work to correct itself and the weight creeps back on. The human body is conditioned to keep on weight for survival and protection from malnourishment, especially for women, since we are responsible for reproduction of the human species. Childbearing affects our bodies, no doubt. We have to work to get our post-delivery bodies back in shape, which is made more challenging because our stomach muscles stretch during childbirth and don't always come back! (It's called diastasis recti.) I say this is all a small price to pay for the gift of giving birth.

And then there's the "S" word: Stress is a huge factor when it comes to losing weight. Some people lose weight when stressed but most of us tend to pack it on because we reach for food as solace. Yet we don't have to ingest anything yummy to feel the detrimental effects of stress on weight gain. Just the *thought* of going on a diet releases the stress hormone cortisol and immediately slows digestion, so you are starting at a deficit from the outset; and chronic stress can absolutely keep that belly fat from disappearing. The "willpower muscle" is the one that wears out first when we're stressed. Let's face it: If you're dieting, you're already hungry so when that sneaky blood sugar drops, you're likely to grab anything that's not nailed down. You know the helpless diet drill: Little or no breakfast, a light lunch, and by mid-afternoon you're inhaling every snack in your pantry. By dinner, you've gone rogue, so you might as well eat enough dinner for two people and vow to start anew tomorrow.

> *I've decided I'll never get down to my original weight*
> *and I'm okay with that.*
> *After all, 6 pounds, 3 ounces is just not realistic.*

Food Shaming is Media Gold

Today's media doesn't help matters; in fact, it makes it worse. We are constantly barraged with messages that we're not good enough and need to do more and be more to be valued and happy. Advertisements are filled with models telling us what products and diets we should buy to improve ourselves, and we tend to feel shame if we are less than the media's ideal image. This is ingrained in our culture and has been communicated to us from a very young age. Most of us, therefore, are dissatisfied with our bodies and are all too willing to hop on the deprivation-diet rollercoaster every chance we get, hoping that maybe, just maybe, this time the results will stick. Deprivation leads to binging—and I don't mean "Breaking Bad" on Netflix. We get caught up in the cycle of overeating, feeling guilty, getting depressed and then hating ourselves. Rock bottom hits right after the holidays or a vacation, followed by an even more restrictive diet that accomplishes nothing more than taking a wrecking ball to our metabolism. Shame breeds more eating and the cycle continues unabated. We unconsciously begin to think of food as control. *If I can't control my eating, I am a failure and not disciplined. I am weak.* This then begins to define you as a person. And the beat goes on . . .

The world is too hard as it is without letting your pants have an opinion on how you are doing.

—Anne Lamott, writer

It is striking to me that many times when I get together with friends, the subject inevitably turns to weight. Complaints fill the air like feathers in a pillow fight about how fat and disgusted we feel, or how thin someone else is. I am guilty of this too, as one friend mirrored back to me by saying, "What are you talking about? I just heard you complaining about how fat you are!" That shocked me into silence and I am now fully conscious of my words. Another gal-pal confessed, "I think about food 90 percent of my day." I also recently observed a friend complimenting another on her weight loss and how amazing she looks. While this was true and said with love, I couldn't help but wonder how this friend might feel if she gained the weight back. When your self-esteem is tied to your weight, you are a prisoner to food and calories.

We are not happy with ourselves until we reach the desired goal weight, which may never happen. When did it become "she who deprives herself of the most calories wins?" As I said earlier, what we truly desire is the "feeling" we get from being skinny. This feeling is different for different people. Some need to be super skinny to feel good, some need lots of makeup, some need Botox and cosmetic surgery. Notice where you are on that spectrum and what you need to feel good. Then try and feel good with a little less … and just be who you are. As we will discuss further, it's all a state of mind and you can choose what and how you think.

Just imagine if you could spare yourself the pain and suffering of crash dieting and still achieve your weight loss goals. Imagine if we could conserve the mental and physical energy we waste thinking about our waistline and put it into making ourselves less stressed, happy and content. What if by being mindful and at peace with food and ourselves we not only drop the physical weight but the emotional weight as well? How would it feel to finally get off the roller coaster and stop struggling? The truth is you can, and here's the best part: It will make you happier and healthier, and lighter inside and out.

> *When eating healthy and exercising become who you are,*
> *you're not constantly fighting to maintain your commitment to it.*
> *You begin to love and crave healthy foods and start to move*
> *your body just because it feels good.*

Renegotiate Your Relationship with Food

So, what's the answer? Well, it's not slogging over to the nearest all-you-can-eat buffet. Your relationship with food is the logical place to begin a long-term successful plan because, well, we need to eat to live. Food is not the enemy; quite the opposite. It has the potential to nourish us, give us energy and even make us smart and strong. No matter how you choose to eat—maybe you are sensitive to gluten or want to experiment with a paleo-style of eating—remember that it's your relationship to food that counts because that is what will make it sustainable.

Susan Albers, PsyD explains in her book *Eating Mindfully,* that a diet mentality focuses on the negative—what you can't eat, your bad habits, self-hatred, food as the enemy, temporary time limited eating, and numbers on a scale. Conversely, when you eat for your health, you are focused on food as fuel, self-love, good choices, long-term habits and what you want for yourself. You start eating healthy because you love and respect your body and want to feed it the best possible fuel so that it runs optimally. Self-hatred is what drives us to stuff ourselves in the first place.

Changing your mindset will not only lead to effortless weight loss but will maintain your skin, hair, nails and health, and is way easier to maintain long term than a temporary diet. Mindful nutrition is not about being hungry and feeling deprived. It's about nourishing your body with real, whole foods so that you are consistently satisfied, energized and able to live life to the fullest. That is the definition of good health.

When it comes to food choices, I subscribe to the 80:20 theory: 80 percent "healthy choices" and 20 percent "enjoy yourself" choices. Focus on quality and "real" food versus processed, low-calorie garbage. I would much rather eat a homemade dessert than one with a list of ingredients that I can't pronounce.

Food is not just calories; it's information.
It talks to your DNA and tells it what to do.

—Dr. Mark Hyman

The Case for Good Nutrition

Have you ever noticed that when someone experiences a serious health crisis, such as a heart attack or cancer, they generally shift from eating for weight loss to eating for health? Why? Their perspective has changed. They suddenly understand how valuable their health is and what it's like to lose it.

It's a shame that we aren't more proactive about this, but it's just not how we (or our doctors) are trained (although it seems to be gradually changing). We look to MDs as the ultimate authority when it comes to our health and they are valuable, necessary resources for acute care, surgery and medication. Generally speaking, however, they have little knowledge about nutrition and typically offer only medication to manage chronic symptoms. This is like stepping on a tack, taking Tylenol for the pain, but not taking out the tack. It only treats the symptom, not the cause.

Getting to the core of your chronic issues is crucial for long-term health and it all starts with nutrition. Most chronic diseases like cancer, heart disease, high blood pressure and diabetes can be controlled up to 80 percent by lifestyle factors. Bruce Lipton, PhD, author of *The Biology of Belief*, has done research with two identical DNA samples; he found that when he put them in different environments, they responded differently. This means that the environment in which genes live makes a difference in how they are expressed. We are no longer believed to be victims of our genetics and we do have more control over our health than we might imagine—although I wouldn't go so far as to completely agree that our beliefs can radically change our DNA, as Lipton suggests.

CASE STUDY:
Good Digestion = Good Health

Karen was having stomach aches and digestive issues when she came into my office. She wanted help with relieving her symptoms through proper nutrition, as her GI doctor only offered medication and testing (and the recommendation that she lose some weight). Her diet consisted mostly of cereal with milk for breakfast, sandwiches for lunch, and pizza or meat for dinner.

I suggested that Karen change up her diet and experiment a bit, like swapping out the processed cereal for a healthy smoothie made up of unsweetened coconut milk, fruits, some protein such as nut butter, and a healthy fat like avocado. For lunch and dinner, I wanted her to try protein and vegetables only, and remove most grains, gluten, dairy and sugar. This anti-inflammatory way of eating was a good way to test what foods were not agreeing with her. Karen was dedicated and able to stick to it.

After a few weeks, her stomach pains subsided significantly and she was feeling much better. We slowly added back in some grains and dairy, but Karen found that dairy was a definite irritant. She could tolerate oatmeal and other gluten-free grains, but pizza was out. Was giving up her beloved pizza really that easy? Well, living without it made Karen feel so good (although she did indulge from time to time, and paid for it with recurring stomach pains). She also lost a lot of weight after being "stuck" for a long time. Her energy improved and she felt amazing in her body. So perhaps going off pizza was not a breeze for Karen, but it is so worth it for her.

Smoothies versus Juicing

I love smoothies. I make one daily in the summertime, mostly for lunch. Most people find it simple and easy to make them for breakfast. If there is enough protein, smoothies can be a meal replacement. There are so many combos and as a superfood junkie, I can fit a ton of nutrient-dense foods in there. Since you put the whole fruit in a blender, you are also getting fiber, which slows down absorption and helps keep you moving. Juicing is great, too, but different than smoothies. You get a high level of nutrients from vegetables, but the fiber is removed (which can cause blood sugar spikes) and it doesn't fill you up. Another drawback is it takes a lot of veggies for a small amount of juice and it can be a pain to clean the juicer. However, juicing provides instant energy and a high level of nutrition to your cells. I'm a smoothie girl but I certainly can't condemn juicing. It's a matter of preference and what works for your body.

Stay-in-the-Moment Smoothie Formula

Here is my secret formula for making power-packed, energy-boosting superfood smoothies:

- **Pick a base**: 1-2 c. unsweetened coconut or almond milk, water, herbal tea, coconut water
- **Pick a fruit**: 1/2-1 c. (frozen or fresh) Berries are great; they are low-sugar and high in antioxidants
- **Pick a protein**: 1-2 T. hemp, flax chia seeds/powder, nut butter, Greek yogurt, high-quality protein powder
- **Pick a fat**: 1-2 T. coconut oil, nut butter, seeds, 1/4 avocado
- **Greens**: (optional, start slow and increase): Up to 1 c. organic spinach, kale, Swiss chard, cucumber (spinach/pear and kale/mango pair well together)
- **Bonus superfoods**: cacao (for chocolate flavor full of nutrients), spirulina, bee pollen, ginger, parsley and dates (to sweeten if necessary)
- **Blend**: with crushed ice and serve immediately.

Jumping On (or Off) the Gluten-Free Craze

Many people are confused about gluten, and rightfully so. The problem with gluten is not wheat itself but how we grow, process and eat it. As humans, we have been eating wheat for 10,000 years, but today's wheat is not the same wheat as even a generation ago. While modern technology makes growing wheat easier and cheaper, the pesticides and chemicals are stronger and more toxic. As a result, many people are experiencing digestive issues with wheat, which is why the gluten-free craze is a craze.

About one percent of the United States population (one in 100) has Celiac Disease, myself included. It is an autoimmune condition that causes damage to the small intestine when gluten is ingested. The body misinterprets gluten as the enemy and attacks itself. Gluten is a protein found is wheat, rye, spelt, kamut, farro (and some oats that are not specifically gluten free). There can be a wide range of symptoms such as stomach complaints to skin rashes to neurological issues, but other people (like me) can be asymptomatic as well. Some people who do not have Celiac, but are sensitive or intolerant to gluten, may notice that they feel significantly better after going gluten-free. The only way to know if this is you; try going gluten-free and see how you feel.

Don't get caught up in the gluten-free trend as a fad health diet or weight-loss approach. If you are eating a lot of processed gluten-free food, which is often high in sugar and calories with less nutrients, you will most likely gain weight rather than shed it. If you are having undesirable digestive symptoms that you and your doctor cannot figure out, you may want to try going gluten-free for three months to see if those symptoms clear up. If they do, then you have a choice whether to go back on gluten and how much you wish to consume.

At the Institute for Integrative Nutrition in New York City where I studied nutrition, I was introduced to the concept of bio-individuality, which means that no one diet will work for everyone. Experiment when you eat certain foods and take note of how you feel afterward. We are all highly individual; for example, some do better as vegetarians but others don't feel as well without meat. Having said that, here are some general guidelines that work for everyone.

Get to Know Your Additives

Make no mistake about it: The chemicals in our food supply are demonstrably dangerous. Artificial colors and flavors have been shown to aggravate ADHD (attention deficit disorder with hyperactivity) and other conditions. A lot of these chemicals and preservatives are banned in other countries but not the United States because the food industry lobby is so strong here. A general rule is if you can't recognize or pronounce the ingredient, it probably shouldn't be in your body. The food industry formulates our food so that we become addicted. They create the right amount of salt, sugar and fat to make sure our taste buds are very happy. Sugar is highly addictive and eventually we lose our taste for real food. Our taste buds have been hijacked!

What's worse, our children are targets as well. One in three children will become obese and this is the first generation of kids that are predicted to have a shorter lifespan than their parents. Adult onset diabetes is not only an adult problem; it is now a childhood disease as well. This is an epidemic that needs to be addressed in the culture at large and also in our own homes and pantries. We have control over what we purchase and consume.

The Terrible Truth About GMOs

Genetically modified organisms, or GMOs, are genetically modified food products that have been intentionally designed for maximum production at minimum cost to the food industry. Most GMO products are corn, soy, canola, zucchini and yellow summer squash.

Genetic modification is a new science and the effects on our bodies have not been determined. Most other developed nations do not consider GMOs to be safe. They also have tight restrictions and bans on them. The United States, however, has approved GMOs based on research provided by the very companies that stand to profit from them.

Pesticides Kill More Than Bugs

Pesticides are quite dangerous and yet completely acceptable for use on our food sources in the United States. This is why I recommend eating organic whenever possible. Every year, the Environmental Working Group (ewg.org) comes out with a list of the Clean Fifteen and the Dirty Dozen. These are the crops that are safest and least safe based on the types and amounts of pesticides used in the growing process. My rule of thumb is that fruits and vegetables with thick skin are safe to buy non-organic, for the most part. But do check the above lists because it isn't always obvious. For example, potatoes are on the dirty dozen but sweet potatoes are clean. (Tip: You can always tell organic produce because the number on the sticker starts with a 9.)

Is Your Gut Leaking?

According to Dr. Andrew Weil, a leader and pioneer in integrative medicine, leaky gut syndrome (also called increased intestinal permeability) is the result of damage to the intestinal lining, making it less able to protect the internal environment. Leaky gut is caused by inflammatory foods like sugar, gluten and alcohol, and toxins such as antibiotics, pesticides, steroids, mercury, BPA and even common pain relievers. Probiotic supplements and elimination of inflammatory foods can ease digestion and heal the gut lining. Leaky gut syndrome can wreak havoc on the body, causing digestive issues, autoimmune disease, allergies or asthma, hormonal imbalances, ADHD, mood fluctuations, skin conditions and Candida. When undigested food particles or bacterial waste leak through the intestinal wall, it may spark many health conditions. Hence, the adage: If your gut is healthy, your whole body is healthy. Functional medicine or naturopathic doctors often treat the gut for all of the above health issues. (Note: medical doctors often don't recognize this syndrome.)

What You Put ON Your Body Also Matters

In addition to the quality of the food that you put in your body, be mindful of chemicals and products you are putting *on* your body. Your skin is the body's largest organ and it's important to realize that these chemicals sink in. Parabens are a common chemical in skin products and can mimic estrogen in the body. "Estrogen disruption" has been linked to breast cancer and reproductive issues. We are not completely sure of how much is unsafe so to be on the cautious side, the less chemicals the better.

Also, be mindful of environmental toxins such as pesticides on your grass, cleaning products in the home, sunscreen, hairsprays and other aerosols that you may inhale. Many companies have paraben-free products and cleaning products without toxins.

You Can Do This

Lifestyle changes are the only way to sustain weight-loss long term and maintain good health. When you detox from sugar and start to eat whole, unprocessed foods more consistently, your taste buds will change and eventually you won't crave—or even want—sugar anymore. Substitute other forms of sweetener and you won't be deprived. Start with raw honey and natural sweeteners like Stevia. They still read like sugar in the body but are more natural than processed sugar and high-fructose corn syrup.

When I was forced to go completely off gluten because of Celiac, I didn't know how I would live without my favorite foods. Now, I honestly have little desire because I have gotten used to what I currently eat. Changing habits is difficult but if we stick with them in a reasonable way, we can sustain them. For most of my life, I loved orange juice in the morning then I switched to water with lemon. For the first few days it was tough but now I crave the lemon water.

Start by making small changes. At first, add things into your diet instead of removing them. Then crowd out the poor choices with more of the good ones and you won't feel deprived and inclined to binge.

You will have to plan your meals more but it's well worth it for your health, weight and energy level.

As an important first step, clean out your pantry and toss or give away as many processed foods as you can. Focus your meals on whole foods, like fruits and vegetables. If you don't like to prepare meals, look for places that make fresh, organic dishes with good quality ingredients. Look for health food stores that sell products with less chemicals, flavorings and processed oils; for example, try lentil and chickpea chips instead of processed potato chips. Gradually take larger steps until your diet is a much cleaner and healthier diet.

The "Pass My Lips" Test List

Before you put something in your mouth, ask yourself (when you can):

1. Is it a whole, unprocessed food in its natural (original) form and not in a box?

2. Are the fruits and vegetables (fresh or frozen) organic? (Big box stores have large bags of frozen organic fruit.)

3. Is the meat or poultry grass fed and organic; Is the fish farm raised or wild? (Wild is better.)

4. If you drink cow's milk, is it organic and *at least 2% fat*? (Nutrients in fat-free milk are harder to absorb and contain added sugar to replace fat) Nut milks (almond, cashew, coconut and others) are good alternatives. If you can, Google a recipe and make your own nut milk. It's simple to make.

5. Are the fats in your diet healthy fats, such as raw nuts and nut butters? The less processed, the better; raw is better than roasted and salted. Seeds like chia, hemp, flax, sesame and pumpkin get a thumbs-up. Healthy fats like avocados (who doesn't love guacamole?) and olives are yummy and healthy.

6. Is the oil you are using unrefined and first-pressed? Use virgin olive, avocado, sesame or coconut; avoid soy, canola, corn or vegetable. Use coconut and ghee (clarified butter) for high heat; EVOO, avocado and sesame for lower temps or on salads.

7. Can I use an alternative flour like almond, coconut, chickpea or rice in place of wheat flour? The Bob's Red Mill brand has many healthy blends.

8. Is this a whole grain that is minimally processed? Try Ezekiel brand bread if you are not avoiding gluten. It's sprouted, high fiber and non-processed.

9. Can I use a natural sweetener such as raw local honey, dates, stevia and molasses instead of sugar or artificial ones?

10. Can I use a boxed or frozen broth instead of canned? Homemade is best.

New Skinny Shopping Tips

1. Shop the perimeter of supermarkets, including the refrigerator, freezer, produce and meat sections, not the inside where boxed processed foods lurk.

2. Buy local and seasonal produce. They are more likely to not be laden with pesticides and trucked from long distances.

3. Frequent your local farmer's markets. It's fresh, close by and social, too; plus, it supports your community farmers who put care and love into your food.

4. Read labels. The less ingredients, the less processed. Know what you are eating! If a product has ingredients that you can't pronounce, don't eat it. Ingredients are listed in order of most first and the least last. Sugar should not be the first ingredient unless it's a dessert.

5. Check Environmental Working Group's (EWG) Dirty Dozen and Clean 15 for the year.

6. Remember that you are voting with your dollars every time you support companies that are organic, non-GMO and treat animals humanely. If enough of us buy these foods, they will eventually become cheaper.

7. Remember that what you skimp on now to save a few dollars, you will pay for later in medical bills. So, think of it as an investment in your future. Look online for discount distributors who sell organics and non-GMO items for less, like Thrive Market and Vitacost. And there is always your local organic market.

The Fab Four... and Four to Avoid

The following four items are mini-miracle workers when it comes to health and staying slim and trim. Each one boosts metabolism, burns fat and detoxifies the body. You can easily incorporate them into your diet right now.

1. **Apple cider vinegar**. It's true. Warm lemon water with a splash of apple cider vinegar in the morning is cleansing and can really help with digestion. ACV has many other benefits, like lowering blood sugar, and is even an excellent skin toner. Try one teaspoon plain in water or in seltzer for a refreshing drink.

2. **Coconut oil** is another multi-use oil that is worth experimenting with. It's wonderful to cook with at high temps and can also be used as a skin moisturizer (it smells like the tropics!). Be sure to buy virgin (unrefined) coconut oil. There has been controversy in the news lately about coconut oil because it is a saturated fat but many of its benefits are backed by science, such as increasing metabolism, building muscle and curbing the appetite. Use in moderation.

3. **Unsweetened goat milk, kefir, kombucha and fermented vegetables** (like sauerkraut) are probiotics and are great for populating your gut with beneficial bacteria. We need these "good bacteria" because Leaky Gut Syndrome (as I point out, above) is becoming more common. I use a splash of kombucha in my seltzer. (Kombucha has a mild alcohol content. I found that out the hard way.)

4. **Dark chocolate** is good for you. Yay! Finally, some good news, right? Look for organic and more than 72 percent cacao (build up to it). The darker, the better. It's a great palate cleanser to finish a meal. High in magnesium, it may help with muscle soreness, in addition to many other benefits. Cacao powder is great in smoothies, too.

You knew it was coming, and here they are: The four foods to avoid most or all of the time:

1. **Diet soda.** Far from being a weight-loss aid, the artificial sweeteners packed in this drink actually make your body crave something sweet. Who needs that?

2. **Artificial sweeteners** (speaking of which) are shown to be harmful and can cause headaches and multiple other adverse health conditions with long-term use.

3. **White bleached flour** (stripped of its nutrients) spikes blood sugar, which leads to inflammation and fatigue.

4. **White sugar** is the biggest culprit of all. It is addicting and leaches nutrients from the body when we consume too much. The intestine rejects it and feeds it to gut bacteria, leading to an overgrowth and damaging cells that inhibit absorption of calcium and magnesium. Bummer, I know.

LET'S MEDITATE:

I'M FED UP WITH DIETING! NOW WHAT?

This meditation will help you shift your mindset from chronic dieter to having a healthier relationship with food.

Listen to the meditation here:

http://www.mindfulisthenewskinny.com

MINDFUL MANTRA:

I will eat to nourish my body.
I need to feel good to look good.

MINDFUL MEMO:

- Change your mindset from dieting and deprivation to eating nourishing foods for your health.

- Be mindful of processed ingredients, additives, pesticides and the quality of the food you're eating and the products you're consuming. Clean out your pantry.

- Think mostly protein and vegetables, nuts, seeds and healthy fats. Limit refined carbohydrates and sugar.

- Try some of the suggestions in this chapter one at a time, and experiment with some new foods.

- Don't overwhelm yourself by making huge changes. Small changes make a difference. You don't have to do everything.

** For a PDF copy of the New Skinny shopping tips, click the QR code with the meditations and download those too!

4

Whoa! Slow It Way Down: Eating with Intention

When walking, walk; when eating, eat.

—Zen proverb

Now that you've killed the die-it, started focusing on real, whole, healthy food, and have given up most (or at least some, I hope!) artificial, chemically processed foods, what's next? Is there a next? Yes, and this is where the fun and fabulous mindfulness stuff comes into play.

Let's go deeper and get into intuitive eating. Knowing when you are hungry and full, and listening to these cues from your body is a revolutionary idea in our diet crazy, over-consuming society. But I can assure you that eating mindfully and focusing on what you put in your mouth, one bite at a time, is a total game changer. By now, you know that I am speaking partly professionally and partly from personal experience. Let me tell you a bit about my journey with food and how I begrudgingly (at first) became a mindful eater.

Believe it or not, my childhood nickname was Junk Food Jodi, and for good reason. Like Lady Gaga sings, I was born that way. The attending nurse in the maternity ward told my mother that I would never be a good eater because I had a tendency to spit out my baby formula. So, there you have it: Branded for life.

Things didn't get any better growing up. I was a picky eater as a young girl. Dinner was often accompanied by not-so-subtle threats from my dad. He would command me to finish everything on my plate by the time the clock struck six in the evening. At 5:59, I'd sneak the undesired food under the table to my overly receptive brother so he could save my butt once again.

Obviously, my poor eating habits followed me into adulthood. (Salad? What?) Then in my mid-thirties, everything changed. As I mentioned earlier, I was diagnosed with the autoimmune condition Celiac Disease and was told by my doctors that I could never eat gluten again. At first, I thought it was some sort of cruel joke. After all, I'd never had so much as a stomachache. Initially, I had gone to a holistic doctor due to a runny nose, thinking I might just have a food allergy, and ended up with full-blown Celiac Disease. Believing this was a hoax, I went to a gastroenterologist, hoping he would debunk this "gluten" theory after performing an endoscopy.

"You have Celiac," he confirmed. "Complete villous atrophy. The villi (small fingerlike projections) in your gut are not absorbing nutrients properly and you need to be gluten-free for life."

You've got to be kidding me. This time I heard it. I was depressed, confused and threw myself a grand pity party. Give up pizza and bagels? I literally mourned the foods I could no longer enjoy. I remember my Aunt Isabel telling me, "It's only food!" That made me feel better for a few seconds. Looking back, however, this diagnosis was a blessing in disguise because it has truly changed my life, and possibly saved it. I learned not only how to eat healthily, but consciously— every last morsel—and in the long run, saved myself from years of sickness. It also directed my career, gave me purpose and introduced me to a whole new way of living.

It was a tough road at first. I had to completely change my attitude and relationship to food. I had to educate myself on what I could and couldn't eat, and why. This was long before the gluten-free craze of today, so the product labeling was a lot more confusing, and basically non-existent. For clarification, I called food manufacturers directly to inquire if a product was gluten-free, and half the time, the customer service reps didn't even know what gluten meant. I scoured every ingredient on every label in search of wheat and other hidden forms of gluten. I was astounded by how pervasive wheat is; I mean, it's in soy sauce, soups, and Twizzlers. Come on!

As for dining out, it became less of a treat. When I'd ask whether a certain entree had gluten, the server usually looked at me like I had three heads; so, I'd ask for the manager, who didn't know much more than the wait staff. Dining out with friends wasn't as much fun, either, although some of them tried to lighten the situation.

"I'll take my pasta with extra gluten" was a common joke among my friends. Other friends called it "fake celiac." At every restaurant dinner, gluten was in the spotlight and it was truly annoying and embarrassing. Even my husband excused himself from the table a few times when I ordered.

Although it was truly a hassle, as I say above, being diagnosed with Celiac was my entrée into mindful eating. Skip the appetizer; there was no warming up to this new lifestyle. I had to go cold turkey, saying so long forever to many of my favorite foods. I had to think about every crumb I put in my mouth, and make sure it didn't touch any gluten. Gluten was the new rat poison. I couldn't eat whatever I wanted, whenever I wanted anymore. Goodbye to food freedom. I had to pause, stop and think before ingesting even a stick of gum or after-dinner mint. Even lipstick needed to be vetted. The good news is that it was a great practice in mindfulness, not just as it related to eating but also my daily habits, patterns and emotions around food.

One Bite at a Time

Mindful eating is not just about what you eat but how you eat it. We're all guilty of polishing off a bag of chips while watching a favorite series on TV or finishing an entire meal without really "tasting" the food. Eating with intention requires us to slow down and savor what's going in our mouths, making sure that it's really what we want to eat instead of grabbing and stuffing out of habit.

It's also a change in perspective about food. Eating mindfully helps repair our strained relationship with food. We eat for the love of eating and the health it can give us, not because we fear it will make us fat. We become grateful for its abundance as we truly notice flavors and savor every bite. We eat when we are hungry in order to nourish ourselves.

Wine connoisseurs have the right idea. They notice every nuance of the vintage they taste test. We can take a hint from them. When you sit down to eat, first "nose" the bouquet of flavors in the food, thinking about where it came from, how it was grown, and even who grew it. Imbibe a small sip or bite and let your taste buds do their magic, noticing the sensations on your palate. Give a swallow and feel it going down your throat, paying attention to the aftertaste. Lastly, notice the finish: how you feel when you eat or drink it.

Mindful eating can be the gift you need to stop the struggle and learn how to eat intuitively. When you slow down your eating, you notice so much more than just what you're ingesting. You learn what you are doing that does not benefit you. You begin to notice your physical and emotional cues for hunger. You can start to understand what emotional issues trigger you to eat when you are not hungry and instead find other suitable outlets for those emotions.

CASE STUDY:
Ali's Holiday Party

It's difficult to not go food crazy at a buffet or party. One of my clients, Ali, struggled every year leading up to the Christmas holiday because she knew there would be plenty of forbidden goodies, including her aunt's famous decadent cookies. We spoke of filling half her plate with veggies, then a quarter protein and a quarter carbs. Ali agreed to bring her own dish to parties so she would have control over its contents.

When it came time for the cookies, she needed a strategy. Ali would usually binge eat a bunch of them and take them home to eat for the rest of the week. We approached this from a "mindful eating" standpoint. She agreed to stop chatting during dessert, and instead mindfully eat two cookies, enjoying every bite. The rest of the batch would go in her freezer for a later time.

With this approach, she wasn't depriving herself that day and she knew she could have a few more at some future point. As it turns out, Ali did not feel the urge to binge and finish them all at once. She ate one cookie every night for as long as they lasted, and she was satisfied. Note: For some of you, just having the food in the house can be a trigger, so know yourself and act accordingly.

Emotional Eating

The tie between emotions and eating deserves a bit more delving into here. Emotional eating is when we turn to food for comfort, stress relief or as a reward, rather than to satisfy hunger. It is all too common. Admit it: How many times have you come home from work or other obligations feeling stressed and craved comfort food? You probably rationalized deserving that meat loaf, mac and cheese, mashed potatoes and blueberry cobbler with whip cream after the day you've had, right? Contrary to popular belief, the antidote for what's making you sad or stressed cannot be found at the bottom of a Ben and Jerry's container.

Learning how to handle stress and emotional eating is important for everyone, yet especially for those who want to lose weight. Once in a while may be okay but using food as a crutch means that you're not dealing with the source of the emotional pain, and one glance at your hips in the bathroom mirror (if you medicate with food on a regular basis) is only going to send you deeper down that rabbit hole.

When your first impulse is to open the fridge whenever you're stressed, sad, bored or lonely, it becomes an issue. Your real emotional issues never get addressed, and the cycle continues, putting on pounds and making you hate yourself in the morning. (Isn't the light in the fridge for night eating, though?) When you feel an urgency behind an action, there is usually something going on underneath. Emotional eating can come in the form of cravings that arise rather quickly, usually are not satisfied, and often involve food that is not the healthiest choice. Identifying your emotional eating triggers can also aid in breaking the cycle. After recognizing the triggers, diffusing the cravings with something other than food can be useful to avoid overeating and weight gain.

Mindfulness can help you identify emotional triggers because when you quiet your mind, you notice what you are feeling. You can monitor emotions and notice sensations in your body as they arise. It also teaches you to pause before you respond, and the same logic applies to emotional eating. Pausing gives you room to see if you are truly hungry or eating to stuff your feelings of being stressed, bored or craving love or comfort.

While eating mindfully 100 percent of the time is not realistic, it's important to do when you know you are going into a situation that could become a feeding frenzy. For example, eating with intention before you overindulge at a buffet is mindful eating. Yet on a regular basis, the idea is to focus on eating when you're eating (not watching TV, reading the newspaper, checking emails or surfing social media on your phone). Having meals is a social activity, so how can you stick to mindful eating during these times with family, friends and co-workers? Simply eating slower will have the added benefits of helping your digestion and improving your mealtime conversations.

Know Your Patterns

Sometimes we eat out of patterns that we don't even recognize. This often results in weight gain that we don't even notice is happening. Self-awareness helps you gain the mental space to reflect on the attitudes, feelings and beliefs that have guided your eating patterns, maybe from the very beginning.

Most of us, for instance, were conditioned from a young age to associate sugary foods with special occasions like birthdays and holidays. Our parents told us that if we were good and finished everything on our plate, we could have dessert. No wonder we associate sweets with celebrations and good times! Examine these attitudes and come to understand them. Listen to what they have to tell you.

Once you begin to notice these patterns, don't react to or judge them. Look at them directly without shame and learn the lessons that your discoveries have to teach you. As I have mentioned, in mindfulness and meditation, we learn to be present to whatever is happening right now instead of trying to change it. This does not mean we have to like what is happening; we just allow it because it's happening regardless. If it's in your current reality, it's best to honestly face it.

Struggle around food usually involves reacting again and again to unconscious triggers in the form of thoughts and feelings. Once we dissect these patterns and create awareness around them, we can pause and create space before we react, thus interrupting our programmed responses. Whereas before, when we'd unconsciously munch until the whole box of doughnuts was gone, now we can choose to look behind the box at what is prompting us to want what's inside it.

"Just Desserts"

My favorite mindful eating time is when I enjoy my favorite dessert at *Le Jardin de Roi* in my town. They offer a gluten-free, almond-flour berry torte that I absolutely can't resist ordering. I do so with intention because I know I am going to savor every bite.

I slow down the conversation a bit when the dessert arrives at the table, and I fully experience the combination of flavors and textures. I don't finish all of it, and always share it with my husband or friends. I do not feel guilty after eating this delicacy. I take pride in the decadence of it. Believe it or not, the way you feel about your food when you eat it does have an effect on weight gain. The mind-body connection between your gut and your brain is how signals get sent back and forth, triggered by emotional responses. Pleasure produces endorphins, which affects hormones, helps metabolize food and stimulates fat burning. So, look at it this way: The more you are getting a positive rush from that occasional special treat of your (conscious) choice, the more fat you are burning!

MINDFUL EXPERIMENT: What's on Your Plate?

Here are some suggestions for keeping your mind on your plate.

- Make sure you are seated whenever you are eating.

- Experiment with eating with your non-dominant hand.

- Intentionally place healthy options in a desirable location for easy access where you will see them, such as on an eye-level shelf in the fridge. Pre-cut the carrots and celery to make grab-and-go a cinch.

- Take some breaths and pause between each bite.

- Eat on a smaller-sized plate.

- Notice what triggers your emotional eating. Pause and check in.

- Notice where your eating behaviors come from. What did your parents convey to you about food and your body?

CASE STUDY: Each Meal, Each Day, Each Choice

Stacy was overweight and wanted to lose the pounds but had given up. I was her last resort, as she was burned out on the diet treadmill. Some diets had worked temporarily until the weight came back… and then some. Stacy seemed to always drift back to grilled cheese and Oreos. She was scared to attempt another weight-loss plan for fear of failure, so she was relieved when I told her that I wasn't going to put her on a diet. After all, what would be the point if she'd eventually go back to her former ways?

At that time, Stacy was rebelling against everyone who was pressuring her to lose weight. It's like she was getting back at them by not trying. Her friends often encouraged her to go for salads or work out with them; they meant well but she resented them for it because in her mindset, they didn't accept her the way she was. They also couldn't understand why the issue of food was more complicated for her. Clothes shopping was especially traumatizing, so she didn't want to have friends come along with her.

The first assignment I gave Stacy was to just observe what she was eating for a week. She didn't have to change a thing; she only had to record her thoughts and feelings before, during and after meals and snacks. When Stacy returned to my office the following week, she reported noticing many things. She observed, for example, that she is a scrounger.

"I'm generally not prepared when I get hungry, so I scrounge around the office or my kitchen at home for food," she explained.

We combated this problem by having her bring healthy snacks like nuts and fruit to the office, and prep vegetables that she could easily prepare and cook for dinner. Stacy also realized that she self-sabotages; she knows what to eat but doesn't do it because she feels it is hopeless.

"My fear is that even if I lose the weight, I'll gain it back, so what's the point?" she expressed.

I assured her that this time was different. Since it is a lifestyle shift and nonrestrictive, she would be able to maintain it long term. We broke it down into each meal, each day, each choice. Stacy noticed she was eating merely out of habit. She was better at catching this at the beginning of the week then lost focus as the week progressed.

Stacy started with small doable changes and went from there. Breaking it down really helped her because she could visualize a lifetime of eating this way and wasn't overwhelmed. Here are a few things that Stacy changed: She stopped drinking soda and added water and club soda with a splash of cranberry to her routine. She started to notice when she had hunger pangs and when she felt full. She made better choices in the work cafeteria, once in a while having her favorite grilled cheese (because not feeling deprived was the goal). Stacy indulged in dessert when dining out with friends, but only if she ate it slowly and mindfully without guilt. Her ratio was 80:20 healthy foods versus "sometimes" foods.

Each day, Stacy began again. Her pants slowly started to loosen on her and she was thrilled. In the midst of our work together, her home scale broke—we joked about that—so she chose to not buy a new one. We used this as a way to increase Stacy's capacity to be uncomfortable and focus on her health and how she feels, rather than the number on a scale.

Although Stacy wondered if she could keep up this "mindful eating" way of life, she agreed that this was much better than the restrictive diets of the past. Now, Stacy is not a woman who does well with being told what to do. Learning how to relate and respond to others that upset her—in a healthy not rebellious manner—was also central to our work together. She told her friends that she had her weight situation under control and to back off!

Stacy developed a trust in me and we eventually looked deeper into her eating issues. Studying the whole picture of her life told me a lot about what works best for her because she was also unhappy at her job and was having friction with her mother. First, we sorted out the job situation then dove into the Pandora's box—starting with untangling the necklace and letting out all that was bottled up, so she could be free and lighter inside as well. Stacy was clinging tightly to buried emotions that were preventing her from dropping the weight. Once Stacy lightened this inner heaviness, she began to shed pounds and feel great. Stacy still has a way to go but the important thing is that she no longer feels like giving up. In fact, she's channeled her rebellion into being a rebel for health!

Five Steps to Mindful Eating:

P: Pause

A: Awareness of emotions and cravings

U: Understand where it's coming from and determine if it's really hunger

S: Slowly savor every bite

E: Excuse yourself from the food so you don't overeat.

LET'S MEDITATE:
MY CRAVINGS ARE OUT OF CONTROL!
RIDE THE CRAVE WAVE

Try this meditation when you are having a craving.

Listen to the meditation here:

http://www.mindfulisthenewskinny.com

MINDFUL MANTRA:

When I have a craving, I will pause before I reach for it and increase my tolerance each time.

LET'S MEDITATE:

I CAN'T BELIEVE I ATE
THE WHOLE BAG OF CHIPS!
EATING MINDFULLY

This is a guided meditation that you can enjoy with our eyes open! Before you begin, make sure you have a piece of dark chocolate, raisin or any tasty small bite of something flavorful nearby (just a piece, not the life-size Toblerone you see in the airport duty free shops). This meditation will help you eat mindfully and with intention. If you do eat something you crave, it will also teach you how to savor and fully enjoy your food.

Listen to the meditation here:

http://www.mindfulisthenewskinny.com

MINDFUL MANTRA:

I will slow down, taste my food
and eat with intention.

MINDFUL MEMO:

- Mindful eating teaches us to slow down, pause, taste our food and not be distracted when eating.

- Get in touch with your hunger cues and what you really want in the moment.

- Notice your patterns, including when, why and how you eat. Where did these habits come from?

- Ride the wave of any craving challenges you are having. Allow it to be there and wait for it to shift. If it doesn't, proceed with mindful eating.

PART THREE:

STRESS REDUCTION/ MIND AND BODY

5

Serenity Now!
Quieting the Mind

You can't stop the waves, but you can learn to surf.

—Jon Kabat-Zinn

Never before in human history have we had so much stimulation coming at us non-stop. We live in a societal culture where smartphones, social media, the Internet and other technology are coming at us at all times. While all these things do have major benefits, they lead to a constant interruption of our attention and distract us from what we are attending to in the moment. We've become a generation of multi-taskers, hopping from screen to screen. Even our screens have multiple screens.

As I sit and write this, I realize that I am sporadically checking email that pops up on the right-hand corner of my screen. My son watches TV while he checks fantasy football, plays games and texts his friends. We call that "triple screening" in our house. A good friend confessed she binge-watches Netflix while scrolling Facebook and answering emails. How many times have you checked your phone out of habit, realizing nothing new has changed in the last 90 seconds? This fractures our attention and leads to an inability to concentrate, which ultimately results in poor performance.

According to a Canadian study on human brain activity, its estimated that thanks to smartphones, we now have a shorter attention span than goldfish. I kid you not. Our attention span has fallen from 12 seconds in 2000 to eight seconds. (Goldfish are believed to have a nine-second attention span.) We are destroying our ability to focus. We are training our brain to need constant stimulation and can barely tolerate boredom or stillness anymore, let alone give ourselves the chance to experience it. Instead, we are fueling our addiction every few minutes. Whenever we have a free second in between running from task to task, we whip out the phone, even when in line at the supermarket, waiting at the doctor's office, waiting for a friend to meet us, or even stopped at a red light. How do we manage all this stimulation, chaos and craziness?

Retraining the Brain

Your mind didn't come with an owners' manual when you were born. If it did, it would say, "Power off on a regular basis to prevent shorting out due to overload."

Neuroscience is the closest thing we have to a documented user manual for the brain. The more we understand how it works, the more we can harness its power to work for us, not against us. Unfortunately, this information is not routinely taught in schools, and although we take much time to care for our bodies, rarely do we pay attention to training the mind. Our thoughts create our emotions, which create our actions. Those actions determine the results we have in our lives. So, our thoughts are what help us overcome any obstacle, accomplish any goal, and handle any stress that comes our way.

Now, let's explore the nature of the mind, how we are wired, and how to effectively master our thoughts to find peace and change our lives. Sound good? I thought so.

The Stress of Evolution

Before we attempt to quiet the mind, we must understand how we got where we are today as a human species. From an evolutionary standpoint, our brains were created (among other functions) to protect us from predators in a primitive environment (that we no longer inhabit). When necessary, this causes us to react appropriately in a hyper-vigilant state. Our innate fight-or-flight response is still extremely useful, but the technology needs an upgrade for our 21st Century lifestyle. Fortunately, most of us don't live in a world where danger is lurking around every corner, but our brains don't know that. Today, we are hunted and pillaged from everywhere and in many forms: environmental toxins, traffic, sedentary jobs, bills piling up, kids needing braces, spouses having mid-life crises, and 24/7 stimulation from countless sources—even from technology we wear on our wrists—which leads to information overload. (Maybe soon we will have a chip in our brains!) Adrenaline and cortisol that were once released as short bursts when we were under attack during our hunter-gatherer days is now constantly flowing because our stress is chronic.

What separates our brain functioning from that of animals is how we process information. When an animal is in danger, it flees then goes back to grazing or resting. Animals are lucky that way; they don't have to concern themselves with trivialities like what the other animals might think of them, or if that little black cocktail dress makes them look fat.

When humans are threatened or perceive stress, we fixate on it even after that threat—perceived or real—is gone. We have advanced cognitive abilities than lesser species have, but this is can be a blessing and a curse. It enables us to imagine, reason, create and analyze. Sometimes it turns to ruminating, obsessing and making up fears and problems that don't exist and may never happen. We can make ourselves crazy with these wild brains of ours (think "fake news" and "conspiracy theories").

The Negativity Bias

Another reason for our chronic stress, from an evolutionary standpoint, is that our brains are wired with a negativity bias. Neuropsychologist Rick Hanson postulates that our thoughts are like Velcro for bad experiences and Teflon for good ones. Over 80 percent of our thoughts are negative.

Again, we've had to be vigilant in order to sense approaching danger and survive, so we are biologically inclined to be perpetually scanning the distance for threats, and we spot them everywhere. The humans in ancient times literally ran to survive; the ones who couldn't move fast enough were killed off. The fast-runner's genes were perpetuated and we've evolved into a humanity that can be quick moving, quite stressed out and even neurotic, at times. Additionally, those who played it safe and were relaxed, who maybe didn't want to disrupt their lunch, often became lunch. Call them optimists if you want, but they are no longer around.

Today, the negativity bias comes out in the form of judgment of ourselves and others, always on the lookout for the negative. I can relate! My husband is nice enough to do the food shopping sometimes and I complain about all the foods he brings home that don't meet my standards. God forbid the strawberries are not organic. He jokingly calls this "food terrorism." I don't mean to torture him! Blame my ape brain!

So, what can we do? Again, neuroscience shows us that we can reprogram the brain so that our automatic response is not one of stress and negativity. We used to believe that once we reached young adulthood, the brain was fully developed and unable to change. Now we have learned this is not the case. Luckily, our minds have neuroplasticity, which means they can change with intervention. Neurons that fire together, wire together; so we need to consciously, and on purpose, manage the stress response as soon as we notice it— unless, of course, there's a grizzly bear near your tent during your family camping trip.

Our Monkey Minds

Now, let's take a look at our thinking process. Our brains are thinking machines and cannot control the influx of thoughts. We have a non-stop "monkey mind" that pings from thought to thought. It is interesting to note where your mind goes when you are not engaged in an activity. This is called the "default mode network." It is this mental gossip that can have a profound effect on your sanity. When your default mode goes negative, it can really affect your mood and emotional state. All that is to say that if we are not aware of our thoughts, they can control us. Author and speaker Sam Harris says, "Thinking is not the problem, but *not knowing* we are thinking is a problem." We get sucked in and actually believe the thoughts. You know what? You don't have to believe everything you think. Thoughts are just thoughts, not reality. It's like "alternative facts" that are untrue because we are making them up.

For example, we make a lot of assumptions about others. If a friend cancels a lunch date with me, for example, my mind (if I allow it) can make up an elaborate scenario that has nothing to do with why my friend actually wasn't able to join me for lunch that day. I may think she's avoiding me, mad at me, had better plans . . . the list goes on. The mind is a prolific playwright, with umpteen story plots all based in fiction. Back in the real world, I find out later that my friend wasn't feeling well, so I would have gotten myself all upset for nothing.

How do we interrupt this constant onslaught of thoughts? Stepping back and observing them in a curious way, like a reporter, can be interesting to say the least, and also help to ease stress. When we separate or distance ourselves from our thoughts, we can see what is happening more clearly and without judgments. It also helps us to shift from stress mode to observer mode, being curious about our thoughts instead of getting caught up in the drama.

Try narrating the story of what is happening without all the opinions. You will soon see a difference. I'll use my example of lunch with a friend: She cancelled lunch. That's it. End of story. No assumptions, and life is peaceful.

As I introduced in Part One, mindfulness can make us more aware of when we get lost in a story that is unnecessary and counterproductive. It allows us to see our way clearly out of the thoughts, and to be present for reality as it is. We cannot stop our thoughts, but we can change our relationship to them. We can choose what we pay attention to and how we respond. This is such a key concept that it bears repeating.

The goal is to have psychological flexibility where you are aware of your thoughts and can adapt to different situations. It is like opening the pores of your mind to new ways of thinking and being. Rigidity of mind can cause us suffering. With a meditation practice, the default mode shifts and becomes more calm and present to sensory experiences and what is happening now, instead of the narration or the story that we tell ourselves.

CASE STUDY:
The Dreaded Family Gathering

During a session, a client named Jen was telling me how mindfulness helped her through a difficult family event. She was going to visit her husband's family for Mother's Day, when she really just wanted to spend the day with her husband and kids. Jen was fine to be with his family, but they had invited many other extended family members that she didn't really know well or have any desire to be with on her "special day." She went to the gathering in a negative state of mind. When she got there, she made small talk but kept telling herself how truly awful the day was, and how she did not want to be there.

Then Jen remembered what she was learning in our mindfulness training. Gradually, she was able to wake up from this thinking and see how her mindset was creating her misery. Her thoughts began to shift. Granted, it was not the ideal way to spend Mother's Day, but she was making it much worse. As the day went on, Jen started to observe herself getting annoyed and watched these feelings without judging. Just the facts emerged: She was simply at a family gathering. The rest was in her head.

As she began to notice this, she intentionally changed her attitude and realized the impermanent nature of the day. She was able to tolerate the situation and even experience moments of joy within it. Jen smiled to herself because she realized that the situation was a perfect opportunity to quietly work on practicing mindfulness. In fact, she remembered me saying to her, "When you are miserable, it's a great opportunity to practice!"

The Gifts of Being in the Present

If you are depressed, you are living in the past. If you are anxious, you are living in the future. If you are at peace, you are living in the present.

—Lao Tzu

Once you learn how the mind works, you can understand why mindfulness is an excellent tool to help manage it. You actually tame your thoughts by being present. When your thoughts are in the past—even if it was 10 minutes ago—you are usually questioning or regretting things that you can't change and just block you from beginning again. This kind of thinking eventually leads to despondency and depression—unless, of course, you are thinking of great memories; but even our glory days can upset us because we can't go back to them.

When your thoughts are in the future, you are usually adding on a scenario that is not going to happen or is based on fear. You then tend to get anxious. You make up "worst case" scenarios. There is nothing wrong with planning or fantasizing about the future, but when you tell yourself fearful stories, you just add a layering of unnecessary suffering. As I mentioned earlier, knowing that they are just thoughts and not reality can help you achieve distance and not feed into the negativity.

The past is history, tomorrow is a mystery, but today is a gift. That's why they call it the present.

What does it feel like to be present, or in the zone or flow? We've all had the experience of being completely absorbed in what we are doing—perhaps playing sports, painting or listening to music—and are so focused that we aren't distracted by our thoughts. I experience this when I play tennis, while my mother gets totally absorbed in her artwork. For each of us, these activities are a form of meditation (which doesn't have to be just sitting on a cushion in a lotus position). We are completely focused on what is happening now because we love what we are doing. Most of us love to eat, so doesn't it make sense that when we eat, we should give it our fullest attention?

Judgment Day

So, if mindfulness is awareness without judgment, let's take a look at judgment in a bit more detail. We are now aware of how harmful judgments toward ourselves can be, but when we judge others or situations and are dissatisfied with the way things are, it can lead to irritability and depression. There are so many things in life that we cannot control. If we are reacting to every circumstance that we don't like, we will be an agitated mess. Learning how to be with what is happening in the moment, can help us let go and bring us peace.

This is a key piece of any mindfulness practice. Suspending judgment means not getting caught up in ideas or opinions, likes or dislikes. It is observing things in a realistic way, which allow us to see things as they actually are. We tend to label everything as good or bad and put things or people in categories based on past experiences. Of course, we are going to have judgments; the key is to be aware of them so they don't cloud our judgment!

A good example of this is traffic. Traffic is simply a bunch of cars going very slowly in a line. When we start putting judgments on it, we make ourselves crazy: *Why isn't this guy moving? Green means go! I'm never going to make my appointment! Honk. Honk.* This is what we all know as road rage. We get all worked up and tense over circumstances that we cannot control. What if instead of making ourselves anxious while in traffic, we took that time to observe our surroundings, like the trees changing colors or the song playing on the radio. What if we just took a breath, give ourselves a break from the craziness outside of the car, enjoy the peace within us and surrender?

Not Resisting What Is

You might think of mindfulness as being passive, but it is not. With this practice, you are taking action on what you can control; what you can't control, you learn to let go. You acknowledge what is happening and don't waste time and energy on "fighting a losing battle." Letting go of resistance is fundamental to one's mental health. You may not like this saying, but in reality "it is what it is." However, it is important to remember another cliché: "This too shall pass." Most things are in life are temporary, so if we are aware of this in the moment, we can tolerate the pain much better. Paying attention to what is happening, even if you don't like it, it instead of fleeing, rejecting or fighting it, mitigates the stress around it. With present moment awareness, you can focus on and become familiar with what you are feeling, which leaves room for you to pause, observe and notice the thoughts, instead of reacting to them.

Mindfulness is not getting somewhere else; it's letting what is here, be here. For example, I hate cold weather, but I live in the northeast so I have to deal with it. I used to curse the snow and freezing temperatures, and dream of being in Florida. Once I started practicing mindfulness, I began to realize that as a result of my negative attitude about winter, my body was tensing up when I was cold. So, I began to consciously relax and just let the cold be there without wishing it away. Did it bring up the thermometer outside? No, but because I am less resistant to it, the cold doesn't bother me as much. I stopped fighting it with my body tension (although, let's be honest, Florida does sound nice).

The Proof is in the Studies

Mindfulness and meditation used to be considered fringe and merely a "feel good" exercise done by hippies and gurus. Now, it has been proven by medical science that it alters our emotional state, which influences hormones, such as cortisol and DHEA, that predict our health. As I mentioned earlier, what we think and feel has a profound effect on the cells of the body and on our weight. How amazing it that?

A Harvard MRI study proved that mindfulness and meditation can actually change the gray matter in the brain, even when practiced as little as 10 minutes a day for eight weeks—although optimal results are gained from 20 to 30 minutes per day. The amygdala (the part of the brain that controls the stress response) gets smaller, so you become less reactive, and the hippocampus (the learning and memory regions, and areas associated with self-awareness, compassion and introspection) increases in gray matter. Meditation can literally rewire the brain! Since this Harvard study, Brown, Stanford, the University of Wisconsin in Madison and many more teaching universities have all done extensive studies proving the effectiveness of mindfulness and meditation. A lecture I attended, given by a Stanford professor, stated that mindfulness meditation is the number one way to physically change your brain without medication. But even science doesn't tell the whole story, as meditation can have a spiritual and metaphysical component to it as well.

• • •

In summary, a meditation practice can:

- Wake you up to your thoughts.

- Allow you to be more open and aware of your current experience.

- Increase your capacity to be uncomfortable with physical and emotional pain.

- Allow you to see with clarity how the mind creates your own suffering.

- Improve focus, productivity, creativity and empathy; and reduce impulsivity, depression, anxiety and stress.

- Result in weight loss due to decrease stress levels and hormones, and mindful eating.

Building the Meditation Muscle

Meditation is not about fixing something that's broken.
It's about discovering that nothing is broken.

—Jon Kabat-Zinn

There are many types of meditation that one can practice, including Tibetan Buddhist, Zen and Transcendental Meditation (TM). I studied Mindfulness Meditation and found that to be what works for me. Professor of Medicine Jon Kabat-Zinn, PhD is credited with secularizing, modernizing and integrating Mindfulness Meditation with science to make it more accessible to the Western world. This method is more than 2,500 years old, but Kabat-Zinn popularized it in 1979 when he studied with Buddhist teachers and realized how beneficial it would be for our society. He designed an eight-week program (Mindfulness Based Stress Reduction) at the University of Massachusetts Medical School to help with those in pain and eventually for others with stress, anxiety, depression and chronic illness.

As you've already begun to experience through the guided meditation links in the earlier chapters, your intention is to focus on your breath. Realistically, your mind wanders and you bring it back— hundreds of thousands of times. When you notice your attention wandering away from the breath, try saying to yourself *"thinking"* and come right back to your breath. This builds awareness of your thoughts and helps you to redirect them. Think of the rep-sets in meditation as attention floating away then coming back, over and over again. The more you do this, the more you build that mindfulness muscle.

You will notice that your brain trails off many times into a series of other thoughts. You may start thinking of what you are having for dinner, or what's on your "to do" list or wonder if you're meditating correctly. This is normal. Think of your thoughts like a train passing by, just don't get on the train. Let me explain this another way. It's like reading the headlines of your emails, but not opening them!

This creates new neural pathways in the brain that will support your efforts to bring about positive changes. The hope is that this may make you more aware of your thoughts throughout your day because in meditation you are constantly interrupting your wandering attention and creating focus.

You may not feel the effects of meditation while you are doing it. To repeat our workout analogy: Much like going to the gym, you don't feel the results when you are working out. Lasting gains come from consistent exercise. It may be uncomfortable and difficult at first, but no pain, no gain!

This passage illustrates the necessity of letting go and how clinging creates our suffering.

Catching Monkeys: An Ancient Parable

They say that in India there is a particularly clever way of catching monkeys. As the story goes, hunters will cut a hole in a coconut that is just big enough for a monkey to put its hand through. Then they will drill two smaller holes in the other end, pass a wire through, and secure the coconut to the base of a tree. Then they slip a banana inside the coconut through the hole and hide. The monkey comes down, puts his hand in, and takes hold of the banana. The hole is cleverly crafted so that the open hand can go in but the fist cannot get out. All the monkey has to do to be free is to let go of the banana. But it seems most monkeys don't let go.

Obstacles to Your Meditation Practice

Once you make meditation a routine, it gets easier. Until then, let's cover some of the obstacles that may come up when you first begin your practice.

- **Sleepiness.** Sometimes the relaxation response is coupled with the sleep response, so we immediately get tired. Notice this and try and stay awake. With time, they will uncouple. Your body may also be telling you that you are not getting enough sleep.

- **Restlessness.** Do you feel the urge to get up or go check your phone? Resist!

- **Anger.** Not being okay with the way things are can lead to anger and feelings of inadequacy.

- **Doubt.** Are you even doing this right? Is this really doing anything? Doubt is very common because meditation may seem too simple and you probably won't feel the effects immediately, as I mentioned above.

- **Desire.** You may find yourself becoming attached to a certain outcome from your meditation, or wanting to feel good. This is the craving mind which leads to fantasies, plans or daydreams.

* * *

In addition to having a formal practice, here are some ways that you can keep your meditation groove going throughout the day.

Informal Meditation: Your meditation practice can be supplemented by an "informal" practice when you are just going about your normal day (whatever "normal" is for you!). When you are in the shower, for example, are you really present in the shower or is your mind thinking about your shopping list, kid's activities, that morning's meeting or a disagreement with your sibling? If you're really distracted, you may even forget if you've washed your hair already. (I'm so guilty of that.) Practice just feeling the warm water on your skin, the soap suds in your hair and the scent of your body wash. For those of you with young kids, it may be your only time alone; don't waste it with your mind pinging from thought to thought. Bonus tip: When you are with your kids, give them your full attention, which will benefit both of you. That is meditation, as well.

This same technique can be applied washing dishes, walking the dog, making dinner, folding laundry, or most importantly, driving the car. All of this mindfulness practice will train your brain to pay attention to what you eat and how you eat it, and will help you stay focused and present in every other area of your life. Get your mind in shape and your body will follow.

I try as often as I can to have a mindful morning routine. I wake up and breathe, pay attention as I brush my teeth, and when I get dressed, I feel my clothes on my body. In these moments, I don't think about the day ahead. Then I eat my breakfast with intention, as slowly as I can—without making myself late for the morning's events.

The Manicure/Pedicure: I went for a mani-pedi one day and decided that I would use this time to practice being fully present. I decided to not look at my phone even once or pick up a magazine. I was just going to pay attention to my surroundings. This was a lot harder than it sounds. Luckily, it was not crowded so no one started chatting with me. I turned on the chair massager for the pedicure and fully focused on the feeling of my muscles relaxing. Wow, amazing.

I noticed my impulse to constantly check my phone, but resisted. I "rode the wave" and it passed. I also wanted to pick up a magazine lying next to me, but also resisted. I used this time as an opportunity to slow down, breath and fully enjoy the moment. I loved the feeling of the massage. I noticed the smell of the nail polish and cleaning supplies. I watched all the manicurists in action, working furiously. I focused on the feeling of having my feet pampered. I really embodied it and felt completely relaxed when I left the spa, instead of frazzled by filling my mind with things that I'd have to do when I left.

How many times do you go for a foot massage, eat a yummy dessert or other pleasant experience and barely recall it happening? We are either distracted in our mind, by others or with some sort of media. We think that if we don't use every moment productively, we are wasting time, when in reality, we are just missing the moment. The more we pay attention and live in the moment, the less stressed we are and can simply experience life for the truly amazing adventure it is. Reminder: the less stressed we are, the less we overeat, hence the lighter we become, inside and out.

MINDFUL EXPERIMENT:
Become the Reporter

- Pick an activity of your choosing and follow what I did while at the nail salon that day. Look for moments throughout your day where you can just be in the moment without distraction. How about in the car, waiting on line, waiting for an appointment or waiting for your children at their after-school events? Use these typically useless moments to bring some space and peace into your regularly scheduled, hectic life. Look around, feel sensations in your body, check in with yourself and be present. One-minute meditations are great to fit in at these times, or if you are stressed and need a "moment."

- Become a reporter on your own life. Comment on what is happening as if you are an unbiased journalist. Just state the facts, without judgment, without your opinions. Name objects in your environment to bring you back to the present. Blue wall, white desk, green grass. What do I see, hear, feel?

- Inhale four seconds, pause four seconds, exhale four seconds, pause four seconds, saying to yourself "inhale" as you inhale and "exhale" as you exhale.

- Do a quick body scan from head to toe for tension. Sit still for one minute without doing anything. See how that feels.

Use the following meditation whenever you want to exercise your mind to improve focus, clarity, be more present and calm the wandering monkey mind.

LET'S MEDITATE:

MY BRAIN NEEDS AN OFF SWITCH!
CALMING YOUR THOUGHTS

This meditation will help you practice present moment awareness and use the breath as a focal point to calm thoughts and relax the body.

Listen to the meditation here:

http://www.mindfulisthenewskinny.com

MINDFUL MANTRA:

I will learn to stay with what is happening in the moment and notice it without resistance.

MINDFUL MEMO:

- The mind's nature is to be overactive and on alert from an evolutionary standpoint so that we can survive. Don't respond to threats that don't exist.

- Realize that your thoughts are not you and do not have to be acted upon or even believed. Learn the difference between reliable and unreliable thinking.

- Learn to focus on each moment without judgment.

- Meditation is simply an exercise to train your brain to focus and interrupt the storytelling that doesn't serve you.

- Practice as much as you can in order to strengthen your mindfulness muscle, up to 20 minutes each day for maximum benefits. Five to 10 minutes is great to start.

- You can practice informally by focusing on whatever task you are doing in the moment. When you are washing the dishes, for example, focus on the water and sensations of the soap.

6

Feel the Burn:
Processing Your Stress

We all have stress but the way we respond to it makes the difference.

You've no doubt heard some of these silly yet catchy comments:

"Stressed is desserts spelled backwards."
"If stress burned calories, I'd be a supermodel."
"STRESS = Shit to Remember Every Single Second."

The truth is, stress is hardly a laughing matter. When emotions become trapped in the body because we don't want to feel them or deal with them, it can lead to disorientation, poor judgment and disease (disease). Yes, stress over the long term can literally kill you.

So, what can be done about it? We can't avoid things that make us anxious, tick us off or cause us to worry to the point where we just want to pour a deep glass of merlot and make it all go away for a few hours. The trick is to learn how to properly process and respond to stress. It's all about your relationship to it!

This begins by being better connected to your physical body, as you can receive a lot of insight by tuning into it. Stress may be generated in the mind but lives in the body. In other words, most of us live from the neck up and never pay attention to how stress manifests from the neck down. We walk around with hunched shoulders, tight muscles and racing hearts without even realizing it. Learning how to relax your body results in calming messages being sent to the mind. (The mind-body link goes both ways: Just like the mind can affect the body, the body can affect the mind.) Paying attention to and getting to know these physical sensations are crucial to kicking stress in the butt. So, let's begin.

The Stress Response

Stress occurs when a threat is greater than your capacity to deal with it, and this can include overwhelming emotions. Not all stress is harmful. Acute stress, which is temporary, can motivate us toward things that need our attention and move us to action, in addition to warning us to find safety to avoid threats.

As we've discovered, the fight-or-flight mechanism is there to protect us, but we have built-in defense mechanisms to threats that may no longer exist. We all have had that close call where we almost hit the car in front of us and all systems are activated. What are the physical sensations that you have felt in these situations? When we encounter stress—whether it be acute, like someone following us in a dark alley, or chronic, like financial problems—our sympathetic nervous system kicks in. This is what happens as a result:

- The heart and lungs accelerate so you are able to run faster and respond more quickly to danger.

- Hearing decreases and vision increases so you can focus.

- Muscles strengthen and can result in super-human strength.

- Cortisol, norepinephrine and adrenaline spike and wreak havoc but are there to alert you to become more awake and focused.

- Heart rate, blood pressure and blood sugar increase and blood vessels constrict.

- Possible weight gain, as the digestive energy is focused elsewhere. Blood flow shifts away from non-crucial areas (digestion) to focus on areas needed to respond to a threat (muscles).

In contrast, the parasympathetic nervous system is known as the "rest and digest" system. When we are in this state, we are relaxed and all systems are running smoothly. Our digestion is at its peak. Crucial to this system is the Vagus nerve, which is that little piece of hardwire that is responsible for the mind-body connection. When the body becomes relaxed, this nerve gets activated. Functions of the Vagus nerve include:

- Sending messages from the gut to the brain.
- In the gut, it increases stomach acidity, affects digestive juices and gut flow, and can increase the risk of IBS and other digestive disorders if it is not functioning well, which is why stress can cause stomachaches.
- In the brain, the Vagus nerve helps control and anxiety and depression.
- Connecting to many organs such as the liver, spleen, fertility, kidney and tongue, to name a few, and contributing to their function.
- Satiety and relaxation following a meal are in part caused by the activation of this nerve.

In short, relaxation causes this nerve to function well, which affects many systems in the body and can bring us good health and a sense of peace. Meditation can help with Vagal tone (getting the Vagus nerve in shape) and shift our bodies from the sympathetic to parasympathetic system. In addition, when you meditate, you release "all the feels"—dopamine and serotonin—that counterbalance cortisol levels and bring you a sense of joy and peace.

Get Out of the Head and Into the Body

Nothing goes away until it teaches us what we need to know.

—Pema Chodron

Now that you've gotten a 101 on how the sympathetic and para-sympathetic nervous systems work, let's talk about what happens to the body when we *don't* process our emotions. We've all had times when we were hurt by a friend or family member or felt sad if our child was upset in some way. This is part of the human experience, but it still sucks. Emotional upset and pain are unavoidable; it's how we deal with them makes all the difference.

Being in a hyper-alert state of stress is not comfortable and humans don't like to be uncomfortable. Some of us will run to that shot of brandy, surf the Internet, or distract ourselves in some way so we don't have to feel. Many of us will eat. What this does is bury the emotion deeper, leaving it to rear its ugly head at some point in the future when the same scenario happens again. It may be gone, but it's not forgotten. While some of us suppress these feelings, others obsess and are, thereby, not able to focus on anything else. Sometimes, we cannot let it go and give it way too much attention. Suppress or obsess; either way of coping may be extreme.

What We Resist Persists

As I mention above, when we suppress our feelings, they don't completely disappear. Eventually, this will manifest in other situations when we are faced with similar circumstances. For example, if I step on your toe and you are upset because it hurts, that's logical; however, if three days later, you are still complaining about how I stepped on your toe, it's likely that you had a sore spot or underlying infection there before I stepped on it. Get it? That trigger point had nothing to do with me but I touched on something that had been festering or sensitive to begin with—buried emotions.

I first learned the technique I'm about to share with you at a weekend retreat. The leader asked us to try and make ourselves feel anxious. We sat in meditation conjuring up as much anxiety as possible. When we weren't trying to push it away and allowed ourselves to actually feel the anxiety, it dissipated rather quickly. It was truly an amazing experience. If we sit with our emotions and allow ourselves to drop into our bodies without avoiding it or attaching thoughts, it will pass. Emotions are just energy in motion (e = motion). Simply noticing them creates a shift.

Taming by Naming

Another way that we can diffuse some of our emotions is by simply naming them. Author Dan Siegel calls this "taming by naming." When you name the feelings you are feeling, it can help them dissolve quicker. For example, when you are feeling upset that your husband is working late again, simply note to yourself that you are disappointed. Just by naming the feeling, coming from the observer point of view, you can shift it. It gets you out of the "story" of the emotion.

This can also help your children. When my son would get cranky when he was younger, I'd tell him, "You seem cranky now" or "You seem angry that you can't watch TV now." This helped him to become aware of his feelings, instead of telling him that he shouldn't feel a certain way. (On a similar note, this is one reason why young boys grow up to be men who aren't adequately able to feel their feelings.) Feelings aren't right, wrong, good or bad; they just are. Now when my son acts out, he sometimes says to me calmly, "I'm sorry, Mom, I'm just cranky now." He is in touch with how he is feeling and can name it.

Between stimulus and response, there is a space. In that space is our power to choose our response. In our response lies our growth and freedom.

—Victor Frankl

The Breathing Space

Tuning into the "triangle of awareness" can help us become present in stressful situations and give us some breathing space between stimulus and response. You can practice this as part of a meditation practice or take one minute to do this in the heat of the moment.

The three prongs of the triangle are:
- thoughts
- feelings
- sensations

First, ease the panic by focusing on your breath. This may be difficult at first, so counting inhales and exhales may help.

95

Then notice the thoughts you are having and become curious about them. Is this really true or is there another way I can think about this? Are you stating facts or an opinion? Can you notice them but not get caught up in them?

Next, check in with your feelings. Processing an emotion through the body can help you feel and release it. What do I mean by "processing?" Simply allow the feeling to be there, even though that is the opposite of what your instinct might be. Honor what you are feeling even if you think the cause of your worry may be trivial in the scheme of things. Remember that you cannot help how we feel; you can only help how you think about the situation. So, focus on what you feel in your body, not your thoughts.

Shift out of your head and focus on where the feeling is located based on sensations in your body. Is it in your heart, chest or stomach? Try and describe it. Truly allow it to expand in your body and give it room. It will pass in 90 seconds if you're not "thinking" about the stressor. Finally, begin again.

So the next time you feel angry with a friend or at yourself, get out of your head and into your body. You'll be amazed by how much better you feel after this simple strategy. The goal here is to get out of the thinking loop, begin to feel into the body, make room for it, and allow it to eventually dissolve. At the end of the chapter, we will practice this in a meditation.

The 4 B's can help remind you to:

1. **Breathe**: Take some deep breaths.
2. **Brain**: Check in with your brain for thoughts and feelings.
3. **Body**: Feel it through sensations in your body.
4. **Begin**: Begin again; repeat until you feel a gentle shift.

CASE STUDY:
The Spin Cycle

Casey was 17 years old when she came to me for help with her anxiety. She would, at times, become overwhelmed with schoolwork, friends and all the pressures that teenagers face. When Casey began to get anxious, her thoughts would spin out of control and she'd imagine every worst-case scenario.

We decided to name this phenomenon "the spin cycle." Every time her thoughts would start spinning out of control, Casey acknowledged that the spin cycle was starting up, like a setting on a washing machine. She thanked it for coming and warning her but understood that they were just thoughts and didn't need to be acted upon.

Casey began to notice that her spin cycle would come in moments of stress and to not push it away but allow the thoughts to be there without making it worse. Casey realized that these were not rational thoughts, but a cycle of panic that happened every time she experienced stress. It was just her body warning her of a danger that did not exist.

Casey practiced breathing instead of panicking and dropped into her body. This got her out of her head as she focused on where in her body she was feeling it. Previously, her heart would race, her chest would tighten and her palms would sweat. When she focused on the symptoms instead of thoughts, they started to go away. Feeling them shifted everything. In addition, by naming this phenomenon, we created awareness that allowed her to separate from those thoughts that created anxiety.

After a short time, Casey learned these techniques and was able to manage her anxiety without further treatment. She graduated at the top of her class and is off to college with a little nervousness and excitement. I have no doubt that she now has the tools for success.

Body Appreciation Moments

Our bodies are true miracles. It is important not to ignore or dismiss the signals they give us, as the body is innately intelligent. Due to cultural programming, our minds are not kind to us when it comes to how we view our bodies. We are overly critical and tend to have negative thoughts and feelings about how we look.

"I wish I was as fat as the first time I thought I was fat," a friend recently posted on Facebook. I'm sure that meme got chuckles but in a way, it's a sad commentary.

We are never satisfied, right? But consider that yes, you can be. It's important to take a moment every day to appreciate how awesome our bodies really are, to start being grateful for them instead of rejecting the parts we don't like or deem unacceptable. Our legs take us from place to place, our necks hold up our heads, our stomachs digest our food, our hands type on computers, and countless other things. They are so much more than flesh and fat. When we give them the nurturing and love they deserve, they serve us in a better way.

I'm sure you've noticed that when you abuse your body, it doesn't perform well. When you over-exercise, eat or drink too much, the body eventually revolts. When we can get in touch and in tune with our bodies, we may not only be able to drop the pounds; we can create an awareness of how we truly feel and live more authentically to who we truly are. So, take time every day for "body appreciation moments" and thank your body for how extraordinary it is.

The benefits of shifting out of our heads and into our bodies are enormous. When we are in touch with our bodies, it's easier to tune into our hunger cues, and learn when our bodies need food or just need love and comfort. Eating when hungry and knowing what your body wants and needs to eat come from listening to your body. Most of us don't even know how to do this. Junk food and overeating were not an option for our ancestors because food was scarce. Because of the overabundance of food in our modern society, we often eat just because it is there.

Listening to the body has the added benefit of helping us hone our intuition, that inner voice that is always right, even when we aren't. You know the feeling when you think someone is looking at you or following you? You have no proof of this; you just know. This is because our bodies know before our heads can even compute. We are energetic beings and can feel vibrations and energy before our brains can process it. Ever notice when you feel good or bad "vibes" from someone? We are feeling the energy.

Turn Toward the Skid

Just like emotional pain, when we are in physical pain, our natural response is to avoid it and tense up. Mindfulness, instead, suggests turning toward the pain, the opposite of what we typically do, and relax the body.

Consider this equation by Buddhist author and teacher Shizen Young: Suffering = Pain x Resistance. When we resist pain and wish it away, or think about all the possible horrible scenarios that will result from it, we make it much worse. We tense up just trying to avoid pain. If we allow the pain to be there and relax a bit, it can shift and dissolve. (Of course, we should ease it when possible with medication, if warranted, and seek medical attention when necessary.) The Buddha has taught us that physical pain is inevitable, but suffering is optional. He compares this to two arrows: the first being the physical and the second emotional. When our thoughts create suffering, it is like we have been attacked twice.

The good news is that meditation and mindfulness increase your capacity to deal with chronic pain. Meditation trains us to not immediately run from the unpleasant, as we've already discussed, but observe it without judgment. Treating our bodies in a kind, loving, respectful manner can actually help.

I had a client who was so angry that she was on crutches because she fell on the ice. She was so resentful and was not getting better with time. She came to me because she started spiraling into depression after a few other challenges came into her life, as well. When she eased up on her ankle and stopped being angry, and allowed herself the space to heal, she started to get better, inside and out. I suggested that she treat her ankle as she would a hurt child and take good care of hers. Again, self-compassion wins the day.

I Like to Move It, Move It

Exercise is important for any weight loss and wellness program, so let's take a minute and discuss it. Although exercise is only 20 to 25 percent of losing weight (it's mostly your diet), it is critical for your health and heart. Yet many people who are told to "go exercise and work out" immediately get stressed at the thought of it.

Ask yourself: Is there some form of movement that you love to do? The more you get into a routine, the more your body will want to do it. Start slow. Don't do more than you're capable of, or you will soon give up. At first, I felt so overwhelmed by spin class but when I stopped comparing myself to everyone else in the class and only competed with myself, I was able to keep going instead of quitting.

To help motivate yourself, work towards a goal. Track your progress and slowly increase each time; you'll feel a rush of confidence as you watch yourself grow. When I really don't feel like exercising, I tell myself to just get there and do 20 minutes, or just do low resistance if I'm spinning. It's all about the routine and doing something is better than nothing. Sometimes that's all I do, but more often than not, I end up going the distance once I get started. If I don't work at my maximum, I still give myself credit for going and don't beat myself up for what I didn't do. Remember that it's your relationship to what you're doing for yourself that matters.

Changing things up can help. For instance, I have a routine at the gym but I also take new classes like TRX or "Align and Define" to challenge myself. Each summer, I freeze my gym membership and try a studio, such as yoga, Barre method or other specialty studios. I also hike, play tennis or bike on a path, weather permitting. The idea is that I'm finding a variety of activities that I actually enjoy, which motivates me to move!

Follow these three steps to help you stick to your exercise game plan, even when you can't find your motivation:

1. **Make a kickass playlist** that you only listen to while exercising.

2. **Check out the real estate.** When you're beginning a new routine, just get to the gym or check out the route you will hike with minimal expectations of your workout. Simply go. If you think you have to work out for an hour of intense cardio, it may be difficult to psych yourself up to go. You don't buy a house until you've gone a few times and felt comfortable there, right?

3. **Make a deposit each time.** Sometimes we don't exercise or eat right because, well, what is the point? Remember that you have to start saving money before you can buy something, so start tracking your exercise and healthy meals in order to feel that it's making a difference. Your efforts will add up and pay off over time. Remember to work toward a goal to see results.

4. **Maximize your efforts.** When you do begin exercising, make sure that you pay attention to your body instead of letting your mind wander. Be present! Yoga specifically focuses on this, as it is a moving meditation combining your body with your breath. When you are lifting weights, focus on the muscles that you are working on. When you are spinning, focus on your legs and the exercise itself. When you are walking, pay attention to your stride, and what you see, hear, feel and smell. Walking my dog is more pleasant and meditative when I leave my phone on the kitchen counter.

MINDFUL EXPERIMENT:
Walk It Off

This type of walking is useful for those who are uncomfortable with sitting meditation or prefer to move during meditation. It might feel strange because we are not used to walking slowly or without a destination, but give it a try. To walk mindfully, take very slow steps, paying attention to your feet touching the ground. Notice your balance; heel toe, heel toe. You may even say these words to yourself. Just silently focus on your feet and the ground and walk a few steps, pivot and turn back around, or walk in a loop. You'll be surprised what you begin to notice. If you are outside, you may also pay attention to the scenery and appreciate the beauty of nature. Try this in your house or out in nature for 15 minutes and see how you like it, then increase your time from there.

LET'S MEDITATE:

I DON'T WANT TO FEEL THIS.
I PREFER RETAIL THERAPY!

This meditation will help you explore how to process your emotional or physical pain.

Listen to the meditation here:

http://www.mindfulisthenewskinny.com

MINDFUL MANTRA:
I will feel the pain so I can process and release it.

LET'S MEDITATE:

I'M TENSE AND DON'T EVEN KNOW IT.
GET TO KNOW YOUR BODY

This body scan can help you connect with your body and the signals it gives you. This connection will also help you tune into tensions throughout your day so you can relax your shoulders when they are hunched or soften your jaw when it is clenched. This meditation is usually done lying down with pillow underneath your knees to support your back. Done before bedtime, it can be extremely relaxing.

Listen to the meditation here:

http://www.mindfulisthenewskinny.com

MINDFUL MANTRA:

When I am stressed, I will pay attention
to my body and release the tension.

MINDFUL MEMO:

- When you notice your body in a stress response, take deep breaths into your belly to activate the parasympathetic nervous system.

- What we resist persists. Feel your emotional and physical pain to diffuse and release it.

- Get out of your head. Allow yourself to get in touch with your body to calm down, develop your intuition and process emotions.

- Pause and find some space between stimulus and response so you can respond rather than react.

- Find enjoyable ways to move your body and pay attention to the physical sensations as you exercise.

PART FOUR:

CHANGING YOUR MIND

7
Reboot!
Resetting Your Programs

Whether you think you can, or you think you can't—you're right.

— Henry Ford

Sometimes in life, we have to go down in order to get up, go backwards in order to move forward, or dig deep so we can grow to new heights. That's the next step in our "mindful is the new skinny" life transformation: uncovering the layers to understand our programmed behavior, beliefs and habits. Understanding the dynamics of how we created our current situations can help us muster courage, break through fears and achieve our weight loss and other life goals.

Many people wait until they hit rock bottom and have no choice but to change. The last straw finally motivates them. But what if you could reserve those straws just for your cocktail hour mojitos and instead avert a major meltdown altogether? Seriously, who needs more drama in life than we already have?

Having an awareness of an undesirable behavior is the first step, as we discussed, in interrupting and therefore changing it. Being willing to look at yourself without getting defensive is the hardest part. We are so accustomed to denying our weaknesses or making excuses for them. When we finally see it, really see it for what it is, the behavior is no longer "automatic." Here is where mindfulness concepts come into play again. Awareness without judgment. Sound familiar? This applies to old programs and habits, too! In order to create the new neural pathways that we talked about in Chapter 5, you may have to cut through some tall grass but in time, you'll see the clearing—and there may even be a rainbow or mango tree there waiting for you.

Tracing the Origin of Your Core Beliefs

So how do you interrupt programs that you've had for decades and core beliefs that were instilled in you from a young age? You have to go back to when you were an innocent little toddler. Really? Yes, really. How come? Well, we are actually born without beliefs and conditioned behaviors. We download these programs from our parents and our environment from the ages of birth through six. Our brains are susceptible in these early years (like it's in a semi-hypnotic state) and they absorb all the information around us. This "data" that we accumulate from the world forms our core belief system.

As children, we want to explore and have little fear of doing the "right" or "wrong" thing. Our parents put limits on us so that we can conform to the society in which we are living and be safe. We are given cues as to how we should play or what we should avoid. So, from childhood we are programmed to believe what society has told us about who we should be and what we should do. Most (or all) of us are fearful to break the mold and often learn to look to others for validation and approval. We worry about what others think, making it difficult for us to go against the crowd mentality and act independently.

This conditioning applies to every aspect of life. Think about how you act around issues related to wealth and money, politics and social justice, religion and faith, family and friends—and, of course, physical beauty. It can be interesting—and quite helpful—to think about where your beliefs originated and start to question them.

If you struggle with eating, think about how your mother, sisters and others related to food and their bodies. Was your mom always on a diet? Was she always complaining about her weight? Did she compare herself to others? What are your beliefs about money? Did money come easily to your family or did you always struggle growing up? What religious beliefs were you taught? Do they make sense to you? Unless we are mindful of what we say and do, we can default into these old programs from childhood, even if it's not how we wish to show up in the world. When we don't pay attention to how we are acting, our autopilot mode goes into effect and old beliefs and habits keep repeating. Once we learn how to change it and practice over and over, the default program can be overwritten.

For example, my client Liz was always quick to yell at her kids. She had very little patience with them and felt horrible about it. When we talked about how she grew up, she mentioned that her mother was always exploding on her. Liz was always on eggshells, never knowing what her mother might get upset about. Liz realized that her autopilot mode was repeating the cycle that her mother began. When she made the connection, she was mindful of the effect it had on her and wanted to make sure she did not continue this behavior. It took time to break the habit and it wasn't a perfect process, but with awareness, her yelling at the kids decreased dramatically.

Becoming aware of subconscious programming and interrupting the habit loop of thoughts and behavior is the goal here. But it doesn't happen overnight. Consider that we think 60,000 to 70,000 thoughts every day and 90 percent are the same ones, over and over (and most of them negative). Our brains have no off switch, so information is constantly "live streaming."

Some of us continually play out our earlier traumas over and over again because we want to resolve them, and it's simply what we know and what we may think we deserve. That is why an emotionally abused child may find herself in emotionally abusive relationships as an adult. Realizing that we are not that scared little kid anymore, and don't need to subject ourselves to the same type of behaviors we were familiar with, is key to breaking the patterns. We all have some emotional dependency needs from childhood, despite our efforts to heal and our parent's best intentions; therefore, we could all benefit from some inner work to prevent long-term suffering, and to reset internal programs to drive change. If you feel that your childhood issues are still affecting you in an unhealthy way, you may want to consult a good therapist to work them out so history doesn't repeat itself.

CASE STUDY:
The Universe Has Your Back

Mary was belittled by her mother while she was growing up, and her sisters were very controlling of her. She never felt smart enough to trust her own choices. Every decision was made for her and when she did try to express herself, she was shamed.

When Mary came into my office for therapy, she was in a relationship with a very controlling man who was demeaning to her. She hated how he treated her and complained about how he didn't value her. Mary had unconsciously sought out a familiar situation, which was replaying the trauma of her past. It was what she knew, expected and was comfortable with, no matter how dysfunctional. She was attracted to this man because he took care of her so she thought he was "different."

Once we shined awareness on the situation, Mary was able to gain the courage to rebuild her self-esteem and realize how the past had affected her. It has been a long process for Mary to trust that she will be okay, but she knows that when she learns to take care of and trust herself, the universe will have her back.

Creatures of Habit

What exactly is a habit? It's when the body becomes the mind, or when the body automatically does an act before the mind thinks it. The body can do things that the mind isn't even aware of when it's on autopilot. Think about it (or don't!): You can drive a car or ride a bike, or maybe you can play a musical instrument, without thinking about the keys and chords.

Another way that habits play out is that we learn to associate cues in the environment with cravings. For example, whenever I bring my dog to the groomer, I immediately crave the peppermint lifesaver that they offer next to the register. Imagine the countless associations that you must have subconsciously made from the time you were a child—all that are now habits!

Meditation can help us uncover the habits of our mind. As I mentioned in the first couple of chapters, meditation helps us see with clarity the nature of the mind. When we can be aware of and observe our thoughts, they no longer become subconscious programming and can be changed. The same logic applies to physical habits. Once we become aware of our unconscious (or conscious) habits, we can change them. We have to intentionally break and instill new patterns. A plan needs to be in place for the new habit to take hold.

So how do we do that? One great way of creating a new habit is to just try the new behavior for a week and see if you notice any difference in your life. I have a friend who always seems to be pulling out his phone and playing games on it every free chance he gets. Without judgment, I invited him to experiment with what it would be like to go one week without the games. I thought this would be non-threatening because I wasn't asking him to do it forever. Although he did not accept my challenge (resistance to change is common and it's hard to get someone to do something if it doesn't come from within them), it would have been a great way to notice how his week could be different. What would he notice? Would he spend more time connecting with family or be more in tune with his surroundings? Think about something you would like to experiment with and give it this try.

Putting a new habit into an already established routine is helpful. If you want to start meditating, plan to do it after something you already do daily, such as brushing your teeth or eating breakfast. Deepak Chopra, MD suggests trying RPM: Rise, pee, meditate. Simply add it to your existing routine. Making props for the new habit to be easily accessible is crucial. In the meditation example, put the timer or cushion next to you bed so you see it; the least amount of steps it takes to get there, the better. If you want to start running, put the running shoes next to your bed instead of buried in the closet. I've even heard of people sleeping in their gym clothes. The research shows it takes 21 days to form a habit, but it takes less time to see if it works for you.

The same logic applies to breaking a habit. Remove the cues and items that enable you. I hate to be Captain Obvious here, but if you're trying to lose weight then get rid of the junk food! It's not a good excuse that you buy it for your kids because they shouldn't be eating it either! And if you must have some junk food in the house for the kids or when friends come over, put it out of your sightline or in another section of the pantry that you don't frequent. Don't make it so easy for yourself to grab something you know is bad for you. I know I've said this already, but if you change what you eat for long enough, that will be what you crave and you will form a new habit. Why? Yes, of course: because we are creatures of habit!

Moving Beyond the Fear

I've had a lot of worries in my life, most of which never happened.

—Mark Twain

Fear is a common obstacle to being able to change. It is usually based on something that we worry about that hasn't happened yet, and most likely won't happen. As I heard spirit junkie and author, Gabby Bernstein say, "It's future tripping." I love the acronym:

False

Evidence

Appearing

Real

I'm not talking about fear that comes over you when there's a burglar in your home. I'm talking about the fear that holds us back and stops us from being all that we can be.

Marianne Williamson, author of *Return to Love,* says that our deepest fear is not that we are inadequate, but that we are powerful beyond measure. The fear is quite often not about failure but rather success. We keep ourselves small so others won't judge us or feel inadequate. But, who are we to not be awesome? Most people play it safe for fear of ridicule, failure and shame. Fear is a natural part of the human experience. Our brains make up all types of scenarios based on fear because we are trying to protect ourselves. If we lean into our fears, as we talked about previously, we know we are going in the right direction. We can allow the fear to be there but not let it stop us.

CASE STUDY:
Giving Up Being Perfect

Trisha is a 40-year-old mom of two boys who came to me with fears of not being a good enough mother and constantly beating herself up—a perfectionist who can never do enough. She had terrible stomach issues due to an Inflammatory Bowel Disease and also wished to lose some weight.

Trisha often found herself crying over little mistakes or stresses and seemed to be a sensitive soul. To make matters worse, she was mad at herself for crying all the time. We worked on dissecting where these beliefs came from and why she felt the need to be perfect.

Trisha desperately wanted to change and be different. We worked on accepting the parts about herself that she didn't like. Once she accepted that she is sensitive and stopped rejecting the part of her that cries, it took away some of her stress. I asked Trisha to treat herself with respect and love instead of berating herself for not being perfect. Learning to forgive herself for missing a school meeting or having a bad morning with the kids was crucial.

When we dove deeper, she came up with the question, "What if I really do like myself?" She continued with this line of questioning: "Then who will I be or how will I act?" She wondered, *what if everything is okay in my life? Then what will I complain about or wallow in? What will occupy my mind?* Trisha couldn't wrap her mind around what her life would look like if she weren't struggling all the time. She had defined herself by this for so long that she could not reconcile a version of herself that wasn't "fighting the good fight." If she couldn't reconcile a successful and peaceful self then would there ever be a "happy Trisha?"

Once Trisha realized all the reasons why she was resistant to change, she was able to accept who she is and what she could accomplish if she let herself. After that realization, there were tears followed by a new level of understanding and compassion for herself.

Going forward, Trisha allowed herself to cry when she needed to, realizing that she is human and therefore not infallible. She was able to let things go and live in the moment. She was even able to drop the 10 pounds she wanted to lose by prioritizing food that made her stomach feel better in order to heal. Additionally, she noticed that when her stress level went down, her stomach upset decreased.

Once Trisha shifted her mindset, it changed the whole ball of wax. She understood that her transformation is about knowing that she is a work in progress and recognizing when progress is being made.

"I know now that it's never going to be perfect," she said to me during her final appointment. "And that's okay because that's not my goal anymore, thank goodness!"

Finding the Courage to Put Yourself Out There

Success is not final, failure is not fatal: it is the courage to continue that counts.

—Winston Churchill

Our core beliefs can also hinder us from being courageous. When I first started my business, for example, I struggled with a belief about myself that I wasn't good at writing or public speaking. But I had to market my business, so how was I going to get my message out there? I acknowledged the fear and did it anyway (as this book proves, right?).

Like we learned from Trisha's story, it's not about being perfect, yet we must start somewhere. My first blog post was a leap of faith for me and I landed in a better place than expected. The editor of a local publication read my post, asked me to expand on it and published it in her magazine. I have been writing for that magazine ever since. If I hadn't put myself out there, that obviously wouldn't have happened. As Wayne Gretsky famously said, "You miss 100 percent of the shots you don't take."

This is not to say everything you try will be successful. For the record, other articles I have written have been rejected. Failure is part of the journey. Just "recalculate" as if you made a wrong turn and try another route. How many times have you heard stories about successful artists, writers and CEOs who all faced rejection before they succeeded?

The same goes for my fear of public speaking, which is one of the most common fears that people have. I could barely speak in a meeting, let alone in front of a crowd. I would turn red and my heart would race. How would I ever be able to speak to large groups? I started by presenting to a group of friends in my basement. Looking back, it seems comical. I was nervous, nauseous and my voice was shaky for at least the first 10 minutes. Yes, I cared what they thought of me but that was my ego talking, the inner critic who always second guesses. When I switched out of ego mode, I realized that I had a message to share and was able to persevere. It wasn't about me; it was about what I could share with and give to others. I expanded out from there and kept going with my presentations. It wasn't easy—and still isn't, at times—but it gets easier, especially now that I begin my workshops with a centering meditation. I do it for myself as much as for my audience!

It takes a lot of courage to put yourself out there, to show up and play the game. As Theodore Roosevelt once said, "It is not the critic who counts; not the man who points out how the strong man stumbles, or where the doer of deeds could have done them better. The credit belongs to the man who is actually in the arena."

Life begins at the end of your comfort zone.

—Neale Donald Walsh

We are comfortable with the familiar and have trouble with change, even if the "familiar" isn't serving us so well. Remember that change is uncomfortable, which is why we resist it. When we try to change, we don't feel like ourselves. We'd rather be uncomfortable and suffer with where we are now. Doing something new or different produces anxiety by its very nature. Our brains have to switch out of autopilot and focus on the new circumstances.

Maybe for you, changing your diet takes a lot of courage. It may be out of your comfort zone to eat more vegetables or give up drinking sugary sodas. Gathering new recipes, shopping in different stores and ordering different foods in restaurants take a lot of brainpower, intention and courage.

What if we try and it doesn't work? What if we can't do it? Giving up foods we love and trying new foods that may not appeal to us takes some courage. On the other hand, being unhealthy may serve you in some way. What would you do if you actually had more energy? What would you occupy your mind with if you weren't constantly complaining and obsessing about your weight? Like Trisha, above, ask yourself: who would you be then?

"No more excuses" can be a scary place to be. Sometimes, we don't know who we are without our guilt, fears, complaints, suffering and sadness. Where we are today is a culmination of past choices and behaviors. If we don't change our programs, then we can be certain to predict our future and it will just be more of the same fears.

Recently, I started seeing a client who is turning 30 and is overweight. She watched all of her friends getting married and feared she would never meet someone because of her size. We discovered in the session that she actually feared losing the weight because then she would have no excuse for not meeting someone. What if she as herself was not good enough? The weight was a good excuse for her staying single. She had to learn to lose the weight for herself and not be attached to losing it for a mate. She had to believe that she would meet Mr. Right at the right time and trust that she was worthy.

The Secret to Success

Working hard for something we don't care about is called stress.
Working hard for something we love is called passion.

—Simon Sinek

Success comes to those who enjoy what they are doing. Granted, we don't all have that luxury but your chances for success will increase if you find what you are passionate about. When work doesn't feel like work, you will work hard effortlessly.

Try to remember what you loved to do as a child. You do not have to be good at everything to be successful. Know your strengths, build on them and then find others to collaborate with to do things you are not as good at. Take small steps towards what you wish to accomplish, rather than looking at the end result and becoming overwhelmed. Everyday just do something small toward your goal. I have to remind myself of that as I write this book!

Whether it's your job or your family, only you can make meaning out of your experiences, and only you can give purpose to your life. If we reframe what we are doing, it can breathe life into an otherwise miserable job. A study was done with cleaning staffs at major hotel chains. A performance survey reflected how they were doing poorly by their managers' standards. They needed to incentivize and give meaning to these employees to increase performance. The company decided to give them heart rate monitors and pedometers to encourage them to "get healthy" while they worked. The results were substantial. Productivity went up and the staff felt better about themselves and the jobs they were doing—a win-win all around.

If all else fails, act AS IF you are already where you want to be. When we are confident and fake it 'til we make it, we can sometimes expedite the trip. Adjusting your body language, making yourself big, like putting your hands over your head in a V before a presentation or interview can be a confidence boost. One of the most popular Ted Talks by Amy Cuddy explains this phenomenon.

When you are confident, others will be more likely to believe in you. It all starts with your perception of yourself. Focus on what you want, not what you don't want. The Law of Attraction is based on like attracts like, meaning if you focus on the positives or what you want, that is what you will bring into your life.

The Buddhist philosophy of not attaching to the outcome also applies to success. If we hold on too tightly and want things for the wrong reasons, it brings stress and frustration. We need to be authentic with ourselves, do what we love and the rest will come when it's time. Celebrating others' successes will also help us succeed. There is enough room for all of us to be successful, so there is no need for jealousy. Those who have succeeded before us can be our inspiration that it is possible.

MINDFUL EXPERIMENT:
Resetting Your
Core Beliefs

- As we discussed in this chapter, how we are programmed as a child can automatically resurface without us being aware of it. Let's examine those beliefs now. Ask yourself: What are the programs and core beliefs that get in my way? If you are not sure, listen to the criticisms of others without taking offense. Is there a shred of truth to any of it?

- What would you do if you knew you couldn't fail? The negative voice appears in all of us and stops us from being our best and accomplishing great things. If failure wasn't an option and everything you do is brilliant and correct, what would you do? What do you really want?

- Ask yourself: What would my life be like if my goals were reached? Really think about and imagine all the changes that would occur if you were successful, both positives and negatives. Are there any surprises?

- Go on an elimination diet for your mind. Pick one habit you want to make or break. It doesn't have to be forever, but try it out for a week and notice the difference. Maybe it works, maybe it doesn't. Be curious without judgment. If we approach it with this mindset, it is not overwhelming. Monitor the results. You can even write down how you feel after you make or break this new habit.

LET'S MEDITATE:

I'M STUCK IN A RUT.
HELP ME MOVE FORWARD!

In this meditation, we are going to break through some negative self-beliefs that are keeping us stuck and unable to move forward.

Listen to the meditation here:

http://www.mindfulisthenewskinny.com

MINDFUL MANTRA:

One small change makes a big difference.

MINDFUL MEMO:

- Your beliefs come from early childhood programs that you were exposed to by your parents, teachers and experiences. Become aware of those programs in order to change behavior.

- Change is uncomfortable and fear is part of the human experience. You have to allow fear to be there, but not let it stop you.

- Emotional and physical habits can be broken with awareness and intention.

- Courage is simply showing up even if you fail, and success comes to those who enjoy what they are doing.

8

Shift Your Perspective: Finding Beginner's Mind

In the beginner's mind there are many possibilities;
in the expert's mind there are few.

—Zen teacher Suzuki Roshi

A university professor went to visit a revered Zen master. While the master quietly served tea, the professor talked about his inner life. The master poured the visitor's cup to the brim then kept pouring. The professor watched the overflowing cup until he could no longer restrain himself.

"It's overfull! No more will go in!" the professor blurted.

"You are like this cup," the master replied. "How can you see things unless you first empty your cup?"

It's true, if we want the view of our life to change, we must empty our cup of all preconceived notions, ideas and feelings that prevent us from receiving the new point of view. We must see things through a different lens. We must remain flexible enough to shift our perspective. This mindfulness technique of emptying your cup invites you to see everything as if you were seeing it for the first time. In the last step, we recognized our patterns and behavior, now let's shift the ones that don't work for us.

Looking at the world with a different approach than what you are used to and getting "out of the box" of which you are usually confined is not always easy. We usually listen and pay attention to information that confirms what we already believe, which is called confirmation bias. Think of the news station you watch. Are you a CNN or Fox News fan? We tend to get our news from sources that are in line with our current belief system. To be more open to other ways of thinking, watch other channels and listen to others' viewpoints on your social media feed so you can try to understand how others think. (Although with news these days, credible sources are important. We want to be open but not misled.)

When we examine everything as if it were new, if we fill our cup with new perspectives without judgment or censoring, we can shift and evolve. Being open and not judging others may be difficult but will benefit your relationships with friends and family, as well as with yourself. This doesn't mean that you will change your point of view, but at least you have seen things from a different angle.

It is really a wonderful way to go through life. Think about your job or your daily routine with the kids. Is it similar every day? (Sometimes I feel like every day is "Groundhog Day.") It may have similar aspects to it but if we come to the day with an open mind, recognize the little nuances and have an expectation that something new and different will occur, it will make life more exciting and less predictable.

We tend to get jaded and see the same things over and over without even realizing it. A client recently told me about a project at work that her group was struggling with and has been working on for days. To her surprise, someone new came in with a fresh perspective and quickly solved the dilemma. I used to be in a girl's poker group and many times when a new member joined, she usually won. Beginner's luck or beginner's mind?

We can often stay stuck because we see things through the veil of our thoughts, opinions and emotions—and not necessarily as they are, with all their potential. This is why two people rooting for opposing sports teams could have entirely different recaps of the same game. They viewed the game through different lenses. Similarly, I remember when my nieces from California were visiting my home during the summer. As I drove them around, they were fascinated by the trees, the beautiful woodsy feel and the lake adjacent to my street. It made me realize and appreciate seeing it through their eyes because I had taken it for granted. Now when I drive around, I appreciate my surroundings. I notice the sun reflecting on the water and see the beauty, which brings more joy and gratitude into my day.

MINDFUL EXPERIMENT:
Change It Up

How many of you have the "same seat on the bus" mentality? I invite you to change things up. We all seem to gravitate to the same spot in our spin or yoga class and might even get upset if someone takes our turf. Try a different spot in the class to gain a different perspective. You may be surprised about what you notice. It's fun to try this with your family during dinner, since we usually always sit in the same place. Notice how it feels different (and the pushback you may get from other family members, like I did).

Oftentimes, we get stuck in our ways of thinking. We have ideas of what we believe will be the best outcome and get stressed over things we cannot control. But how do we know that what we think is always best? Remember that we all have our core beliefs and biases. Life doesn't operate through our narrow lens, and sometimes what we think is a setback could be a wonderful lesson or gift in disguise; so there is no use getting upset over things we can't control. We just don't know all the answers and cannot predict the best outcomes.

For example, my son did not make the travel basketball team one year, which was very upsetting to him; but as it turned out, my husband ended up coaching recreational basketball and he had his best season ever with many of his friends (and a lot more fun)! The scenario that he was so upset about turned out to be a wonderful thing!

• • •

Here is an often-told ancient Taoist tale that will put this concept into perspective for you. What we think may be a setback at the time may turn out to be a blessing. We just don't know.

We'll See: An Ancient Parable

Once upon a time, there was a farmer in the central region of China. He didn't have a lot of money and instead of a tractor, he used an old horse to plow his field.

One afternoon, while working in the field, the horse dropped dead. Everyone in the village said, "Oh, what a horrible thing to happen." The farmer said simply, "We'll see." He was so at peace and calm that everyone in the village got together and, admiring his attitude, gave him a new horse as a gift. Everyone's reaction now was, "What a lucky man." And the farmer said, "We'll see."

A couple days later, the new horse jumped a fence and ran away. Everyone in the village shook their heads and said, "What a poor fellow!"

The farmer smiled and said, "We'll see." Eventually, the horse found his way home and everyone again said, "What a fortunate man." The farmer said, "We'll see."

Later in the year, the farmer's young boy went out riding on the horse and fell and broke his leg. Everyone in the village said, "What a shame for the poor boy." The farmer said, "We'll see." Two days later, the army came into the village to draft new recruits. When they saw that the farmer's son had a broken leg, they decided not to recruit him. Everyone said, "What a fortunate young man." The farmer smiled again and said, "We'll see."

Take the Thick with the Thin

Everything can be taken from a man but one thing: the last of human freedoms: to choose one's attitude in any given set of circumstances, to choose one's own way.

—Viktor E. Frankl

Shifting your perspective on happiness and moderating your expectations of what a joyful life looks like can make you feel lighter and relieve you of a huge burden. It is a misconception that we should always be happy, despite what we might have been taught when we were kids. As children, it wasn't generally okay to be sad or discouraged, and we just had to get over it or keep our chin up. Our parents' first instinct was probably to try and fix our problems immediately, and they may not have understood that our tantrums were very real to us. Who would blame them? It's difficult to see your child sad or upset.

The idea that life should always be happy is a ridiculous notion, because life is hard and not all moments are joyful, nor should they be. Happiness is a fleeting feeling. Instead of reaching to be happy all the time, maybe we should strive to have the full range of emotions and experiences. That is a more realistic plan. In the spirit of mindfulness, not pushing away our sadness, allowing it to be there and expecting that we will have ups and downs is all part of being human. After all, isn't it insane that we truly expect to have a drama-free life? If we let ourselves be sad when we need to and honor the feeling, it will pass.

The suffering comes when we are upset with ourselves for being sad and try to push those feelings away or swallow them down with a big plate of delicious but often empty calories. I had a patient who was depressed but functional. She was so relieved when I told her that it was okay to be sad and to give herself some compassion around it. I told her to think about her depression as if it were a physical illness that she needed to recover from and that it was okay to take it easy. Once she allowed herself to be sad, it took a lot of pressure off of her and she actually felt better.

Remember that e-motions are "emotions in motion." They are all temporary, such as the nature of life. The law of impermanence means that all things in life are temporary. Your body is temporary, your pain is temporary and, yes, as I mentioned earlier, your happiness is temporary. We can't hold onto anything, good or bad. Becoming comfortable with uncertainty and realizing that all things are temporary will ultimately help reduce stress and anxiety.

It's true: Life can be difficult. No one is exempt from life's inevitable times of pain and heartache. How we relate to that suffering determines our quality of life. We can come to recognize that it is the nature of existence to have tragedy and pain. Acknowledging that fact instead of denying or being surprised by it can ease the blow. That doesn't make the pain go away but knowing that we all go through it can help us cope.

MINDFUL EXPERIMENT:
What Movie Are
You In Today?

In order to distance yourself from the little stresses of everyday life, look at your life like you are watching a movie. Don't try to change the outcome of the movie, just simply watch each scene go by. You may feel emotions during certain scenes or even cry. Movies come in many different genres and your life is no different in all its drama. When you are experiencing a strong emotion, think of it on the big screen. Sometimes you're starring in a drama and things can get complicated. Sometimes life resembles a comedy when it is lighthearted, or a tearjerker when sad things happen. It is all part of life, so embrace each "scene."

You may also think of life as chapters from a book, with your age as the chapter number. Everything constantly shifts and changes, so this chapter is only temporary. Who knows how the next chapter will go?

I remember when my son had to get stitches when he was 11 years old. I did the above exercise and realized that this was only a chapter in my son's life, just one part of the book. As long as he was okay, one day we would look back on this as a memory, say 'Chapter 11' and soon he would be onto the next chapter. It helped me put things in perspective and I was able to stay calm in the hospital with him. It really works!

Bigger, Better, Best, Bested

If you don't get what you want, you suffer; if you get what you don't want, you suffer; even when you get exactly what you want, you still suffer because you can't hold onto it forever.

— Dan Millman

In addition to being raised to be happy, we are also bred to strive for more, bigger, better, best. Many parents demand that their children get good grades, excel at sports, have lots of friends and always be on top. We are raised feeling that we are not good enough if we are not winning.

This pressure to succeed breeds insecurity and the result can often be a divisive or nasty behavior with a winning-at-all-cost attitude if taken to the extreme. Healthy competition is important but it bids us against each other instead of unifying us. The American culture is all about success, drive, ambition and being the best. I saw a post on social media recently that a mom would give her daughter a phone, but the condition was that she earn all A's in school. No pressure there.

We are raised to believe that more success will bring us happiness but once we achieve that success, we set the bar even higher, so it's never enough. We think we will finally be happy when we lose 10 pounds, land our dream job, or get our kid into Harvard. The broken formula of "when I succeed, then I'll be happy" is backwards and unattainable. *Learning to be happy with what we have now is the actual key to happiness.* The race to the top is a race to nowhere. And all this busyness can lead to depression, anxiety and tons of stress.

Many young moms who come and see me are looking for their purpose and feel less than because they are not working outside the home. I felt this way, too, when I had young kids. What these moms fail to realize is that there will be plenty of time to work and feel productive in society, but right now is such a short window when they can enjoy their babies. Believe me, it flies by. I have perspective now, which I did not have then. Now I know, all in good time.

This vicious cycle also applies to weight gain and loss. We think we finally will be happy when we fit into our jeans or look amazing in that little black dress. But somehow, we never quite get there and even when we do, we are never quite skinny enough.

A friend of mine just lost 15 pounds and looks great. When I told her that, she said, "I need to lose 10 more." We can still focus on the imperfections if we choose to. It is never, ever enough. That is why we have wound up as a culture of yo-yo dieters, with wrecked metabolisms and pervasive obesity. We are being bested by our own impossible definitions of what skinny means and what is actually best for us.

CASE STUDY:
That Lovin' Feeling

Susan was overweight when she came to my office. She had recently been looking at old pictures of herself when she was much thinner but not necessarily happier. Susan wanted to lose some weight but was not willing to go back to a time to when she ate no carbs and was miserable. She could also recall that the thin version of herself was still not satisfied with her weight, so why go back there?

Susan was smart enough to realize that the deprivation and loss of some weight was not the answer to her problem. Eating healthy and feeling comfortable in her body was her goal. The pleasant side effect of loving herself and eating for nourishment resulted in a slow but steady, natural weight loss and a happy Susan.

The most helpful advice that I gave Susan was permission not to starve herself and enjoy healthy, nutrient dense foods without obsessively counting calories. When you come from a place of shame and pain with your weight, you may be super motivated to lose it but, as we discussed, your body may eventually put it back on anyway. Having self-compassion and feeling good inside was Susan's new goal.

Reframe Your Annoyance

If we are not grateful for what we have, what makes us think we will be grateful for what we want?

Instead of always searching and grasping for more, more, more, gratitude allows us to appreciate what we have now. Cultivating joy requires building the gratitude muscle as part of our daily and weekly workouts. Only in this rep-set, we ditch the wishing, complaining and striving, and refocus on noticing what is going well in our lives right now, no matter how small or seemingly insignificant.

Learning to be grateful for life's simple pleasures can certainly improve your mood and perception of life. I recall a day when my kids were small and I was taking them to get haircuts. Once in the car, my two adorable, precious children proceeded to fight like two alley cats in a scrap yard. As I drove along and listened to this free-for-all in the back seat, I would occasionally interrupt with a "Stop it!" or "Enough already!" When that didn't seem to be effective, I started to get annoyed and then, for some reason, amidst all the noise and frustration, I just gave up.

As the boys continued to yell and exchange insults at each other, my mood turned from annoyance to amusement. It struck me that these two little boys were not going to be young forever, and I realized how lucky I was to have these daily moments with them, no matter how stressful. This total re-frame of the situation filled me with gratitude and the rest of our outing was not just tolerable, it was fun. (The same goes for the mess in the house. When they are all grown up, you will miss that, I promise-enjoy it while you can.)

Gratitude brings us joy and turns what we already have into enough. Instead of striving for the next goal to bring you happiness, appreciate where you are right now. If it's not your ideal place, remember that it's just one chapter in your life's story. Keep in mind that everything changes eventually and you have more power to shape your life than you might imagine. As we've discussed, you can literally rewire your brain and refocus your attention on the good things. This can take time but let's just say that gratitude is contagious. Once you catch the gratitude bug, it replicates itself and even more joy streams into your life. So, how do we cultivate this all-important skill? Here are some ways to begin.

MINDFUL EXPERIMENT:
Gratitude
Journals and Jars

- A gratitude journal is a great way to hone your skills. Every morning upon waking, think of five things you are grateful for, big or small—from your husband's promotion to that cute coffee mug that says "World's Best Mom." This will help to reprogram your brain to scan for positives instead of negatives.

- If you don't have time for a gratitude journal, try sticky notes with affirmations or thoughts of encouragement next to your alarm clock or the bathroom mirror. It can simply say, "Thank you for this new day full of possibilities." It will put you in the right mindset for the day.

- A gratitude jar is great, especially with kids. Write what you are grateful for on a piece a paper every day and put it into a jar. Read these when you're sad or whenever you want a pop of inspiration.

Stop Protecting Yourself from Joy

Live life like it is rigged in your favor.

—Rumi

We are built to protect ourselves from pain and, in the process, we don't live fully. Brene Brown wrote in her life-changing book *Daring Greatly* about the concept of "foreboding joy." We don't allow ourselves to fully love or live because if things go too well, something bad might happen. We are waiting for the other shoe to drop. We want to protect ourselves from loving too much because if something happens to our loved one, our hearts will be broken. We don't fully immerse ourselves in a life we love because it can be taken away in an instant; so, we rehearse tragedy in our minds.

LET'S MEDITATE:

WHY CAN'T I BE HAPPY?
FINDING JOY IN A BUSY WORLD

This meditation will help you retrain your mind to scan life for the good, instead of always looking for something to fix or focusing on what's wrong in your life.

Listen to the meditation here:

http://www.mindfulisthenewskinny.com

MINDFUL MANTRA:

I am grateful for all that comes. I will try and see new possibilities with fresh eyes.

MINDFUL MEMO:

- Use beginner's mind when approaching a situation or conflict.

- Acknowledge that life encompasses a full spectrum of emotions and expect that there will be good and bad times.

- Realize that having the mindset that "when I succeed, I'll be happy" is backwards and unattainable. Learn to find joy in the moment.

- Being grateful is a great way to reprogram negative thoughts and cultivate an appreciation for everything in life.

PART FIVE:

RELATIONSHIPS AND FORGIVENESS

9

Develop Nutritious Relationships: Handling Conflicts

The biggest communication problem is we do not listen to understand. We listen to reply.

—Stephen R. Covey

We are inherently social creatures with a desire to belong to a community. Sure, eating healthy, exercising and managing stress all contribute to our weight loss goals and overall well-being, but how do our interpersonal relationships affect the same?

Scientific studies bear out that social connection improves our physical and emotional health and decreases stress and anxiety, while loneliness has a detrimental effect on our health, including shortening our life span. We want social connection more than the prestigious job, the sporty car, the fit bod. Actually, it is the reason why we want all these other things. We want to be loved and accepted!

Social connection can happen in a variety of ways, not just the ones that you might expect. All relationships are special in their own way, whether it's with your spouse, children, neighbors, extended family, friends, or people in your community who provide many wonderful services to you—from your dry cleaner to your local barista. Our social circles bring us support, enrichment, shared history, companionship and even love. Since we need others in order to flourish and thrive, it is worth looking at our relationships and investing in how to maximize them to the fullest.

Is Your Relationship Nutritious
or Full of Empty Calories?

Healthy relationships feel good and as the Beach Boys famously sang, you can feel the "good vibrations." Ask yourself if a particular relationship fills you up with love and respect or is toxic and draining. At some point in our lives, we all have that one friend who brings us down but who we can't seem to let go. Even if you know that a relationship isn't necessarily good for you, it can be difficult to extract yourself. A casual acquaintance is certainly a lot easier to distance yourself from than a parent or spouse.

Setting clear boundaries with those with whom you are tied to is necessary to continue to stay healthy. You cannot change others but you can change the dynamic by modifying your own behavior and perspective. Our families are our greatest spiritual teachers. When author Elizabeth Gilbert was asked, "How come your family knows how to push your buttons?" she responded: "Because they installed them." They are always challenging us to rise to the next level and become more skilled at dealing with stress and conflict. Just when I think I am so "mindful" or super-Zen, my sons often remind me how much work I still need to do.

"Breathe, Mom," they reflect back to me, when I start to get upset with them. I may get defensive at first but I know they are right.

In triggered moments, we can pause and ask ourselves what lessons can we learn from this and what is needed right now. Patience? Dignity? Compassion? We can choose to take responsibility for how we respond to these button-pushing attempts, even if it means removing yourself from the conversation.

Ask yourself the following questions about your relationship and listening skills in order to become mindful of your interpersonal habits and how they impact all your relationships.

Relationship Skills

- Do you pay attention to your actions and words or act on autopilot without much intention?

- Do you react immediately when something triggers you or do you pause before you respond?

- Do you assume you know what the other person is going to say or act before they say or do it?

- Do you accept others for who they are or do you really wish they would change?

- Are you grateful for the partner or friends you have or do you find yourself constantly searching for more and better?

- Do you give to expect something in return?

- Do you judge people instead of trying to understand how they see the world?

- How do you handle criticism from others and are you highly critical of others?

- Do you find yourself distorting the truth a bit in your conflicts instead of just sticking to the facts?

- Do you ask for what you want and need, or just hope the other person will give it to you without verbalizing or modeling it?

Listening Skills

- Are you fully listening when someone is talking to you or are you daydreaming and distracted?

- Do you tend to jump in and give people your advice right away?

- Do you have the need to argue?

- Do you need to constantly be right?

- Do you change the subject when it seems threatening or uncomfortable?

- Do you placate the other person and agree with them too easily?

The following concepts can be useful in improving the nutritional value of our relationships, rather than starving yourself of the emotional nutrients you need to live and thrive.

Pay Attention

Husbands are the best people to share secrets with.
They'll never tell anyone because they aren't even listening.

Paying full attention to your actions is an important step in reducing conflict. Bruce Lipton, PhD describes the following phenomenon in his book, *The Honeymoon Effect*. Think back to when you were first in love. The adrenaline was pumping, you were glowing, and you didn't need sleep. You ran on pure love. You showed this person your best self because you were actually paying attention to how you acted and were fully present. You wanted them to see the best parts of you and were able to hide the "crazy." This was your conscious mind at play, creating your wishes, desires and intentions.

Then the relationship progressed and you felt more comfortable with this person. You went back to your "normal" life and the usual stress we all have, which took some attention off this relationship. When you stopped paying full attention, the subconscious "autopilot default mode" kicked in and that's when the person could see the "real you." This actually isn't the real you; it's the programming that you downloaded from all your past experiences and information. It's what we reveal when we stop paying attention.

Obviously, we can't pay attention to our spouse or anyone else 100 percent of the time, so our actions are on autopilot when we aren't. If I just react to my husband over nothing because I've had a long, tiring day, for example, I am on autopilot. I would not intend to act this way on purpose. In addition, paying attention to the words coming out of your mouth is also important. Be aware that your words have an impact on others, and even yourself. Pause and think about what you are saying. This may be difficult as life goes so quickly, but when we speak with intention, we have fewer regrets.

Listen "Mind-Fully"

Another key to mindful communication is fully listening. The greatest gift we can give to someone is our attention. These days, distraction is one of the biggest communication problems in a relationship due to our ever-present mobile devices and other technology. For this reason, it is more important than ever to give others our full attention.

Due to social media, we may have more "friends" but less personal interactions. When sad and lonely, the next generation is learning to turn to their phones rather than each other for support. Social media releases a dopamine hit, much like alcohol, and this is how our kids are growing up! Face-to-face communication is being lost, and the art of "people-watching" is dying. Our society is becoming more divided and isolated instead of fostering more connectivity. Now it's even more important when we disagree with a spouse, co-worker, family member or even a Facebook friend that we fully listen. This means hearing the other's point of view and putting yourself in the other's shoes. This understanding or empathy is crucial, especially if you are strongly opposed to their perspective. Remember that everyone has different ideas based on how they grew up and even members from the same family can have very different experiences.

These days, political conversations seem to be a source of contention for families and our online network of friends. Do you rush to unfriend someone or openly listen to what they are expressing? And yes, sometimes you do have to unfriend or break ties with someone who is simply too toxic or unkind. I have certainly done that at times. But we must try to bridge the gap and look through another person's glasses to find a way to understand and relate. Trying is what it's all about. Remember that beginner's mind!

Happy Wife, Happy Life

This is all easier said than done, you might be thinking. For sure, relationships can be tricky. We can go from infatuation stage to "how did I ever marry you" as quickly as we can say "I do." A happy relationship depends on many factors. We come into them with baggage and expectations from the culmination of our past experiences. We model our relationships based on our parents because they are the only marriage for which we had front row seats. This doesn't mean you are doomed if your parents' marriage failed; we also learn what we don't want in a marriage by observing others.

You've probably heard it said that we often unconsciously look for a partner who has qualities that we don't have ourselves, thus making us feel whole or complete. "My better half", we may call our life partner. This makes sense and our spouses can be our "opposite." (Yep, opposites attract.) The day may come to pass, however, when what originally attracted you to your partner can end up being an annoyance. "He's so neat and picks up after himself so well" can morph into "He's such a neat freak! I leave one spoon out on the counter and he flips out!" Again, we see through our narrow lens and if our partners do not conform to our ideas of a good spouse, we tend to get stressed and angry.

Embrace Imperfections and Be Generous

So, what can we do about this? Well, while I have seen couples in my therapy practice, I'm not a marriage counselor and this isn't a *Men are From Mars* type book, but I've learned a thing in my 20 years of practice and have some practical wisdom to impart.

Wabi Sabi is a Japanese concept based on the wisdom and beauty of imperfection. It postulates that there is a crack in everything and that's how the light gets in. Just as we are imperfect, so are our relationships. Embracing this is key to a happy and healthy partnership. We typically think that other relationships are better than ours and often compare, no thanks to Facebook! (Although, I often wonder if the overly mushy gushy posts are truly an accurate barometer of a relationship.) The grass may seem greener but only because you're not focused on growing your own lawn, right?

Accepting your significant other for who he or she is, imperfections and all, is not easy to do. We all have faults and have to face this reality if we desire a healthy relationship. It is really our perception of them being faults that make us unhappy because we wish that they were different. We can only change ourselves, and the way we can possibly change others for the better is by changing *our* behavior. If you know your spouse tends to be testy with you upon arriving home from work, know that and don't take it personally. Not engaging with the behavior and letting the storm calm all by itself can resolve the situation. You have a choice: you can engage in an argument or let it pass. When you engage, you probably end up getting mad for a while. If you are mindful, you are aware enough to not get triggered and take the bait. Additionally, if you respond in a way that he might not expect, it throws him off (in a good way) and changes the dynamic. Try it!

Focusing on the good parts of the relationship and showing gratitude to your partner will obviously improve relations. Redirect yourself to what is going well in the relationship. When you have expectations of what you think you should be getting or experiencing, it kills the gratitude and leaves you unhappy and frustrated. All we really want in life is to be seen, validated, wanted and appreciated. When I feel an impulse to complain about something my spouse did or did not do, I try to think of the good he does and appreciate that (not easy at times, but it's a process). Sharing that with him makes a huge difference in our marriage. Even if I don't catch myself right away, when I realize I'm doing it, I apologize and admit I was in a crappy mood.

Being generous in our love relationships is another key ingredient. The highest and best place we can be in a relationship is to be the giver, without expectations. The beautiful irony is that when we give love free of conditions, we receive the most benefit. Make sure that you are open to receiving those benefits, though.

The key is really "seeing" and paying attention to each other, because when we don't connect, we start to seek out other ways to be seen and get attention. This obviously doesn't help the marriage and can lead to infidelity. If you are struggling with feeling unseen or find yourself checking out of the marriage, seek support or talk to a therapist or skilled coach. Couples therapy is usually a good option if your partner is willing.

MINDFUL EXPERIMENT:
Acting Out

You can't change anyone else but if you change your response to someone, it will have a ripple effect. So, let's experiment with a new way of being in order to shift the dynamic of your relationship. Imagine that you're an Academy Award-winning actress. Now think about a common argument that you have with a spouse, child or friend. How do you typically respond in these situations? Now mindfully, with intention, plan a new way of responding. It doesn't have to be forever, just see what happens this one time. Use your beginner's mind and your ability to pause before you react, and respond in a different way with an open mind, non-judgmentally. Did the other person react differently? Did you change the other person by changing yourself? Were you able to avoid a conflict? Did that make your life easier? If it worked, continue to mindfully respond in that way. If not, experiment with a different way until the desired effect is achieved. (I know you may have to be the bigger person here, but it's worth it in the long run!)

Model the Behavior You Desire

Modeling what you want from the other person is a more effective strategy than always asking for what you want. We may complain that our spouse isn't doing something but are we doing it ourselves? Sometimes we make assumptions that our partner knows or understands what we want or need, but they do not.

Being clear about what you want and showing them what kind of behavior you want by acting that way yourself can be helpful. If I want my partner to be more affectionate, I shouldn't demand that behavior from him; I should show him. I can verbalize what I want, but it is up to me to initiate affection if that is what I desire, not rely on him.

What we focus on grows. If we are focused on the good and appreciate aspects of our partners, then they will naturally show more of the desired behavior. Demands never work and just alienate the other. Become the person with whom you would want to be.

Just like you, your partner has limitations and you cannot expect them to fulfill every need. Understanding this and seeking others to talk to about certain things that your partner cannot relate to or have interest in is important. I set myself up for disappointment when I expect my spouse to care about a topic or go with me to an event of which he has no interest. We can't expect to be everything to everyone.

Marriage joins two people together but remaining independent is important, too. You really don't have to do everything together. One reason why my marriage works is because we let each other do our own thing without guilt. My husband, Lewis, has his poker game nights and plays golf. I have my girl's nights, workshops and retreats. If I really want to go somewhere and he doesn't, I go. This healthy independence allows us to not harbor resentment and keeps us both happy.

Your Spouse is Your Mirror

Realistically, when you live with someone for years and years, even decades and decades, there are going to be arguments. Remember that the people who trigger and upset us can end up being our greatest teachers. Think about it: There is a reason why we react to some things and not others. What may bother me may not bother you at all. We can learn what our deep-seeded issues are based on what really bothers us. Usually it is an old hurt coming back to haunt us.

When your spouse criticizes you, instead of being defensive and dismissive, listen next time. It may be a bit of an exaggeration but most likely there may be a shred of truth to what is being verbalized. If we are able to listen without our ego getting involved, we can view it simply as information instead of a personal insult. It is usually a clue to what triggers our behavior and what we are doing. Spouses are our mirror and can teach us about our unresolved conflicts from childhood and into adulthood. Constructive criticism is helpful; contempt can ruin a marriage. Verbal abuse is never acceptable.

Marriage can be challenging and takes a lot of work and attention. If we think it will be perfect, we are in for a big surprise. Knowing that we all are struggling to a certain extent can be reassuring. Reframing, as I discussed earlier, is a wonderful technique to use when thinking about relationships or your current situation. We can't always choose what is happening in our lives but remember that we can chose how we think about our lives. If we are coming from that grateful place, we can see the positive aspects of our circumstances.

CASE STUDY:
The Brady Bunch

Sara came to me because she was unhappy in her marriage. She had gotten remarried when her two girls were in middle school. Her new husband had two sons that lived with him, so they essentially became the Brady Bunch minus two kids.

Adjusting to this new situation was difficult for all. Sara felt powerless when it came to decisions around the home. Since she was living on his turf, she did not want to make any waves. Eventually, one of her daughters ended up moving away and had little contact with the family. Sara started to blame her husband and their situation for the friction she felt from her daughter. Sara also blamed her husband for being complacent with her needs. He was not a good communicator and she found it difficult to voice her opinions. It seemed like everything was on his terms ever since she moved into "his" house.

Now that the kids are older, he is trying to change, but she feels it is too late and has a lot of resentment. We talked about her taking some responsibility for her part in this situation. She did marry him with the hope that he would change. Additionally, it was her responsibility to take control now, despite the past. When family history was explored, we uncovered that Sara's sister was narcissistic and treated her poorly. Her parents often didn't take her wants and needs seriously. Her ex-husband didn't respect her. She was repeating old patterns. After some exploration, she really just wanted to matter!

Once she realized this, she knew she needed to shift her behavior. Sara set boundaries with her sister, who was still treating her poorly. Then she took what she learned and became more assertive at home. She began to clearly communicate her needs and concerns with her husband. At the same time, she was more understanding of his limitations and adjusted her expectations. She started making her own decisions instead of waiting for him to approve. She was finding her voice.

For instance, Sara wanted a dog but knew her husband would not help with pet care. As soon as she owned the responsibility and didn't expect him to pitch in, she was able to get the dog knowing that it was all on her. She began to accept his limitations and not take them personally. She knew she couldn't or shouldn't wait around for him to change. Once she accepted this, she became much happier. She knew he wasn't Mr. Perfect, but the dynamic between them improved as a result. She even started showing compassion for him because she knew he wasn't inherently able to be who she wanted him to be, although he was trying.

Soccer Moms or Mean Girls?

Why is there so much drama with moms and girlfriends? Sometimes it seems like the "mean girls" days of high school are never truly over.

How do we deal with friends and "forced friends" (known as your children's friends' moms) and keep calm and carry on?

When it comes to mothers and their kin, there is nothing more protective than a mama bear. This protective mechanism is evolutionary to keep our children safe, but nowadays we have taken this to a whole other level—sometimes, at the expense of our friendships with other moms. My young mom clients have story after story about how other moms have wronged them in the interest of their kids, and it's not cool. One soccer mom lost many of her friends that she had since her son was in pre-school because he made the "A" team and was bragging about it to the other boys. Without so much as a discussion, they turned on her. The kid's hurt feelings about what team they made translated into competitiveness and defensiveness. Ultimately, 10 years of friendship could not withstand elementary school soccer.

Another mom was constantly upset because her child was continually left out of the mother-orchestrated play dates. Some moms feel the need to organize groups of friends to make sure their children are in the mix. What they may not realize is that others are being left out, and that other moms see right through this behavior. What leads a mom to make their child's friends for them is typically driven by insecurity and fear that their child will be the one left out. In therapy, I worked with this client on not personalizing this behavior; because she was brought back to the feelings that she had in junior high school. In a flash, she was back to being the last one picked for the team and left out all over again. Nowadays, social media can amplify being left out for all of us. And when our kids are left out, it's 1000 times worse.

Be Aware of Your Judgments

I have addressed judgment (especially of ourselves) many times in this book, as it is critical to leading a joyful, mindful life. However, judgment of others is equally important. Not only can't we change others but we are often in other people's business, imposing our viewpoints on them and thinking we know what is best for them. Byron Katie, an American speaker and author who teaches a method of self-inquiry known as "The Work," says that when we are judging or thinking someone else should be doing something, we are in *their* mental business—much like, she continues, if an earthquake or snow storm happens, we are in God's business. It is important for our sanity to stay in our **own** mental business. Can we really know with 100 percent certainty what is best for another person? We may know them but are we considering the whole picture? What don't we know? What would happen if they changed? Would that upset the whole apple cart and might that result in other behaviors?

Since we cannot know with total certainty how another should act or be, maybe we can let go of how we think they should be; after all, it's causing us stress. (Katie recommends asking yourself, "What would it be like for you without the thought or judgment?") Additionally, we can look at the judgment of others and turn it around because what we judge in others is usually something we don't like about ourselves.

What's more, we cannot attach ourselves to certain outcomes of situations because we really don't know what the future will bring. We may think, for instance, that our child should get into a particular college and we might be devastated if they do not. Odds are they will go where they are meant to, and more than likely it will all work out. If not, then they were not ready, and will adjust accordingly. Not everyone follows a straight path to success, and it's usually not too late to make adjustments. Letting the universe decide takes a lot of pressure off of us. The belief that something bigger is at play improves our relationships and gives us a sense of inner peace. Remember, "We'll see!"

CASE STUDY:
Insecure Supermom

Jennifer has three children and is always striving to be the perfect mom. She is constantly trying to fix any problems her kids are having. She wants the best for them. It's only natural for parents to want their kids to be social, do well in school and be athletic.

Jennifer worries about her fifth-grade son because he doesn't get asked to many play dates, is preoccupied with Minecraft and video games, and doesn't seem to have many friends. She encourages him to make friends and invite them over. During our session, we worked on her anxiety and fear of him not having friends and how it reminded her of her own childhood and insecurities. She only has so much control over the situation, and while it's great to encourage him, she needs to be careful to not add pressure and just accept him as he is. Jennifer is making a judgment that being social is how he should be, and it may make it worse that she is forcing relationships that he is not ready for or interested in. Not accepting him for who he is and trying to change him brings stress on them and their relationship. He needs to know that he is accepted and loved for the way he is.

MINDFUL EXPERIMENT:
Is It Really True?

- Next time you are in a conflict, write down the thoughts you are having about it. Tease out what is really true and what is your judgment or opinion. Can you notice how your thinking distorts reality and change up the thoughts to match simply the facts? Notice how you feel calmer after this exercise.

- Think of a quality that irritates you about your significant other or someone you love. Can you find a way to embrace this imperfection? Try and remember if it's something you used to love about the person, and try to get back to that place in your mind and heart.

LET'S MEDITATE:

WHY CAN'T WE ALL JUST GET ALONG? FINDING EMPATHY

In this meditation, we are going to focus on accepting others the way they are.

Listen to the meditation here:

http://www.mindfulisthenewskinny.com

MINDFUL MANTRA:

I will embrace the imperfect
nature of my relationships.

MINDFUL MEMO:

- Be a role model for what you want in a relationship.

- Beware of judging others and stay in your own mental business.

- Notice your communication style and blocks you may have to fully listening.

- When in a conflict, notice your thoughts and make sure they are facts and not opinions or assumptions that you are taking personally.

10

Forgive Selfishly: Cultivating Compassion

Holding onto anger is like drinking poison and
expecting the other person to die.

—The Buddha

Congratulations! You've made it to the last step. What a journey it's been! You have learned the "greatest hits" of mindfulness and meditation along with concepts that will give you a new perspective on your life and the challenges you may face. We have covered self-care and being kind to yourself, healthy and mindful eating habits, shifting your mindset and how to experience true success in your relationships and your life.

Now it's time for the *piece de resistance*, and I'm not talking about dessert. It's time to sample the highest goal of mindfulness: spreading loving kindness and cultivating compassion. Once we learn to forgive ourselves and ditch the negative inner critic, as we have talked about in previous chapters, it then becomes easier to give others the same respect and kindness. Coming from a place of self-compassion, we are now ready to extend that to others. It's time to pay it forward.

Bringing loving kindness into your own heart then out into the world will have a huge impact on how you treat others and how they treat you. As we have learned, everything starts with you. Being kind to yourself makes life a whole lot sweeter yet giving kindnesses to others will ultimately benefit you as well.

Forgive Selfishly

Now is the time to finish cleaning out any remaining gunk inside, and I'm not referring to your refrigerator (although now is as good a time as any for that as well). Let's take a look at any grudges that you are still holding. Are you not speaking with a sibling or parent? Is it time to let go of the fact that your friend forgot your birthday? Whether it is a longtime grudge or a petty grievance, holding onto the anger and not letting go of the pain mostly affects you, not the other person. For this reason, letting go of what you are holding onto can be freeing and essential to your lightness of being. By contrast, when we don't forgive, we are holding onto anger that can cause us stress, misery and possibly disease. The emotional weight can affect us inside and out. When we hold on, we are heavy all around.

Sure, when someone wrongs you, it can be difficult to forgive. You become angry, hurt and disappointed. This is completely understandable and it's normal for these feelings to surface. Feeling them is an important part of the healing process but when we hold onto them at our own detriment, then it's beyond time to let them go. It may make us feel good for a time to be angry, but in the end, we are only punishing ourselves. The offender has probably moved on, while you are still suffering. Forgiveness is a difficult process but you need to remember that you are doing it for yourself, not for them. Forgive selfishly.

When you forgive someone, you are forgiving the person, not the act. You do not have to condone what they did or excuse them for doing it. It merely means that you don't hold onto the anger anymore, and you understand that people make mistakes and are human. The closer you are to someone, the more opportunities there are to screw up. Part of the human experience is to allow another to hear what you have to say and for you to be able to hear "I'm sorry" and let it go. You are not letting them off the hook; you are letting yourself off the hook. Nelson Mandela famously forgave his captors. He realized that they did what they thought was right, and if he didn't forgive them, he would still be in "prison." Forgiveness gave him true freedom. Would you rather be right or free?

People Don't Usually Set Out to be Assholes

A wise man once said, "There is no need for forgiveness if we have a deep understanding of others." You may feel that you don't have an obligation to understand the motivation of those who wronged you, and you don't; however, understanding may diminish your hurt. Conversely, when the offender understands your pain, it validates you and can be very freeing.

Usually when people hurt you, it's more about them than you. People do crazy things to make themselves feel safe, sane and secure, but most of the time they don't really intend to be assholes, to be frank. Maybe it's what they felt they needed to do at the time for their survival or status. It may be all they know with the experience and information they have been given. It may be the best they can do in a particular circumstance but it is rarely about *you* so resist the tendency to personalize it.

It is one thing to feel hurt, but we can add a layer of suffering on top of it with our thoughts. The stories we make up around the hurt can absolutely make things worse. Remember that negativity bias in our brains? It can create stories that are not real, only based on our opinions. Don't make assumptions that you know the whole story around what happened!

CASE STUDY:
Angry Gabby

A client named Gabby was always angry at her mother. Her mom never knew how to be a good mother and was never emotionally or even physically there for her. Her mother was very tough and even shaming to her, never making her feel good enough.

I asked Gabby what her mother's childhood was like and she didn't know. When she investigated this and realized her grandmother had bipolar disorder and was abusive to her mother, she was able to begin to soften towards her. This didn't mean that Gabby condoned her mother's behavior, but she was able to understand where it came from and see it through a different lens. Her mother was probably doing the best she could, based on her own experiences and information she was given. That knowledge enabled Gabby to be nicer to her mother, helped her understand, and not be as hurt by her mother's behavior. Rather than coming from a place of blaming and shaming her, she realized that it was not personal at all; therefore, she could be more compassionate toward her. It is also important to note that even though her mom may not have had bad intentions, it didn't wash away Gabby's hurt and pain; it just helped her make sense of it all.

* * *

To demonstrate compassion in action, I will share a famous story in which one puts another's need above his own personal commitment and learns to adapt to a situation that demanded his assistance. In the story, one monk was able to stray from his strict vows for the greater good. The lesson continues because he did so without holding onto guilt, regret or disappointment and was able to move on quickly to embrace the present moment. In contrast, the story of the other monk shows another way of coping by holding onto angst and not letting go of the other's actions.

Two Monks and a Lady

Two monks were making a pilgrimage to venerate the relics of a great saint. During the course of their journey, they came to a river where they met a beautiful young woman—an apparently worldly creature dressed in expensive finery with her hair done up in the latest fashion. She was afraid of the current and afraid of ruining her lovely clothing, so she asked the brothers if they might carry her across the river. The younger and more exacting of the brothers was offended at the very idea and turned away with an attitude of disgust. The older brother didn't hesitate and quickly picked up the woman on his shoulders, carried her across the river, and set her down on the other side. She thanked him and went on her way, and the brother waded back through the waters.

The monks resumed their walk, the older one in perfect equanimity and enjoying the beautiful countryside, while the younger one grew more and more brooding and distracted, so much so that he could keep his silence no longer and suddenly burst out, "Brother, we are taught to avoid contact with women, and there you were, not just touching a woman, but carrying her on your shoulders!"

The older monk looked at the younger with a loving, pitiful smile and said, "Brother, I set her down on the other side of the river; you are still carrying her."

 MINDFUL EXPERIMENT:
The Fast Track to
Forgiveness

Practice these seven powerful steps towards healing your relationship with another:

1. Find and acknowledge the hurt.
2. Observe the behavior without judgment.
3. Remember that accepting doesn't mean condoning.
4. Give the person a break and understand that we all are doing the best we can with the resources and experiences they have.
5. It's more about them than us. People don't set out to be hurtful; it is usually a consequence of them protecting themselves.
6. Validate the person's pain that is behind their behavior.
7. Empathize with the person even though you don't agree with the act.

Don't Make Assumptions

Everyone you meet is fighting a battle you know nothing about.
Could a greater miracle take place than for us to look through each
other's eyes for an instant?

—Henry David Thoreau

I love the quote, "Don't judge my story on the chapter you walked in on." You never truly know what someone else is going through, and if you knew the person's whole story and background, you may feel differently. It is so easy to judge others without understanding the full picture.

There is a story circulating that is often told at mindfulness retreats about a dog that was incessantly barking and the neighbors were becoming incensed. One of the neighbors was so angry he got his shotgun and while he didn't intend to kill the dog, he was going to scare or try and warn it. Who knows what can happen when you're in a rage with a shotgun in your hand? When he went outside to look for the dog, he was shocked to find that the dog's leg was stuck in the fence, probably for hours. The man immediately put down his weapon and freed the dog's leg from the fence. He immediately went from being angry and potentially violent to being a savior and hero for this dog. When we don't have the facts, we may act impulsively and cruelly. The Buddha said that unskillful acts come from ignorance. It's best to refrain from anger or judgment if you don't know the whole story.

I have a similar story that made me glad I was able to pause before I reacted. One time I was parking and a girl in the back seat of the car next to me hit my car with the passenger side door. I was upset. The girl's mother did not say anything to her or me, and seemed to pretend like it didn't happen. When the mother was closing her car door I said in an irritated voice, "Your daughter just hit my car with her door." In a shaky voice, she asked me what I wanted from her. I said, "Just an acknowledgement that she hit the car and an apology." The woman apologized and then proceeded to yell at her grown daughter. I immediately felt bad that she was now yelling at her daughter; I just wanted her to acknowledge it. I said, "You don't have to yell at her, it's not that big a deal." There was no visible damage.

She replied that her daughter is autistic and needs to learn proper behavior. In that moment, I was so relieved that I did not make a scene or get angry at them. I had no idea her daughter was autistic, of course. I would have never wanted to upset her or make an assumption about this young girl. In the preceding moments, I did let my mind go to the negative, thinking she was just a spoiled kid who didn't care about other people. Quick judgments can make you act in ways that you wish you could take back. When you get to know and understand a person or situation, it makes all the difference.

I love the show "Undercover Boss" and the end of each episode literally brings me to tears. Why? Because you have CEOs going undercover, working in the trenches with their employees, getting to know what they do for the company and how it's going. In each scenario, the boss usually gets to know the struggles of the employee that he or she is training under, professionally and personally. This creates understanding and empathy for someone they would have not otherwise known or interacted. By the end of the episode, the CEO reveals him or herself to the employee and usually promotes them, gives them a trip, pays for tuition or gives them a cash bonus if they are doing a good job for the company. Instead of making judgments about their employees based on their social and economic differences, they got to know them as humans, heard their struggles firsthand and, as a result, developed empathy, compassion and a desire to help. The whole world should learn lessons from this show. I can't get enough.

Compassion Makes the Heart Grow Stronger

The greatest degree of inner tranquility comes from the development of love and compassion. The more we care for the happiness of others, the greater is our own sense of well-being.

—Tenzin Gyatso

Compassion is the ability to feel the suffering of another person and the desire to alleviate it. The Latin roots of the word compassion are *com*, which means with, and *pati*, which means suffer. So, the word compassion literally means to suffer with. We are actually born with the innate capacity for compassion; however, we are ingrained to be competitive instead. It can be seen as weak in our society to be compassionate. As Rihanna sings, "All of my kindness is taken for weakness."

When we have feelings of caring and love for others, we actually feel better. We reap a greater reward internally when we give rather than receive. When we practice compassion, we have more strength, peace and joy that transfers to everyone with whom we associate. The more compassion we have for others, the more kindness and affection we will obtain. In addition, compassion spreads from one person to another. When you are compassionate toward others, they are more likely to be compassionate toward others as well. There is a ripple effect. When you pay it forward, like paying a toll or someone's check at the local coffee shop, you are making others willing to do the same. Plus, you have the capacity to make someone's day!

Loving kindness—or as Buddhists say, *metta*—is a practice that cultivates compassion for ourselves and others. This practice is done by first wishing yourself safety, health, happiness and a sense of ease, and then wishing the same to others, some you love and some you don't, and some you don't even know. It begins with you because if you do not love yourself, how can you extend that love to others?

The words "loving kindness" can put people off because it may sound weak, mushy gushy or lovey dovey, but it is a practice that brings us many benefits by changing how we relate to others. When we focus on the good in others, it gives us a sense of connection to all beings and the world. We don't feel as alienated and alone. We begin to realize that all humans want the same things in life; more joy, less pain and a sense of belonging, knowing that we are all doing the best we can. Although people don't always know the most skillful way to get what they want and need, nonetheless we all do want these same things. Basically, we all bleed red.

Three C's to Remember:

1. **Compassion:** for yourself and others… always.

2. **Community:** utilize the support of your friends and family and lean on them when needed; meditate in a community and seek out like-minded peeps.

3. **Commitment and Consistency** (okay, that's two C's but they are very similar): Make a commitment to your meditation practice and be consistent. Build that muscle through repetition!

Intolerance is Based on Ignorance

We have beliefs that have been passed down and taught to us without question. We believe stories from books that are thousands of years old. This is all well and good, but it gets out of hand when we don't tolerate people who don't have the same beliefs as us or look different. If we knew their stories and got to know them as people, our feelings may change.

Ignorance prevents us from accepting one another. Religion can divide us, while spirituality may unite us. With spirituality, we are all one, coming from the same source. We all have the same desires: to be happy and live with ease. By trying to bypass our egos that separate us and finding our true nature, our soul, we have the capacity to be a peaceful people. Ohio Congressman Tim Ryan, who wrote the book, *A Mindful Nation*, states that meditation and mindfulness have the capacity to potentially change the country. This could be what the country and world need right now—to see everyone as human, and have a deep understanding and compassion for all people.

Feeling connection to all humans is the key to this practice. The essence of how we see each other can make us feel more love, compassion and empathy for others. It doesn't mean we have to like everyone or agree with the way people go about their business. It simply means that we recognize them and know they struggle just like we do. Seeing others as human, even if you don't know them well, can make a big difference in your life, as well as theirs. We are all vulnerable beings whose lives can change in an instant; no one is immune. Random acts of kindness to strangers or acquaintances spread quickly. We all can do our part to change the world. It starts with you.

* * *

You may not see the results of this compassion practice right away, but stick with it, the results will slowly emerge. Maybe one day when you do something klutzy, you won't rush to crucify yourself. The same goes for me, and now hopefully you!

At a family gathering, a new mother asked my sons, ages 18 and 15, to tell her one thing I taught them so that she could use the advice when raising her new daughter. My son Alex replied, "No matter what happens, I know my mom will always love me." My other son Brian said, "I can always talk to my mom about anything." Having two adolescent boys, you never know what messages will get through to them (or what they will say). Although I was surprised by their responses, I am so grateful that my compassion has given them comfort. I hope that this will help them to grow into adulthood with compassion for themselves and others. I wish for them to always feel worthy no matter what, as I have learned for myself.

LET'S MEDITATE:

PEACE OUT AND SPREAD THE LOVE!

This meditation guides us through the practice of forgiving ourselves and sending compassion to others. See what feelings you notice as you go through this exercise.

Listen to the meditation here:

http://www.mindfulisthenewskinny.com

MINDFUL MANTRA:

I forgive myself and others and
wish peace and ease for all humans.

MINDFUL MEMO:

- Forgive yourself!

- Forgive others! Forgiveness doesn't mean you condone a certain behavior; it means you are cultivating peace for yourself.

- Try to not judge but rather understand others by hearing their stories and getting to know them.

- Remember that compassion for others makes us more loving, peaceful and healthier beings.

Practice, Practice, Practice

If you can sit quietly after difficult news; if, in financial downturns you remain perfectly calm; if you can see your neighbors travel to fantastic places without a twinge of jealousy; if you could happily eat whatever is put on your plate; if you can fall asleep after a day of running around without a drink or a pill; if you can always find contentment just where you are: you are probably a dog.

—Jack Kornfield

This quote may be a bit tongue in cheek, but it rings true. We can work toward enlightenment and mindfulness but there are no "easy fixes" here, although you may experience a few unexpected miracles as you get to know yourself on a deeper level. As I keep intentionally reiterating, it's called a mindfulness "practice" for a reason. Whatever we practice we get better at, but don't fool yourself into thinking that it will be perfect.

We've already learned that we are not aiming for perfection. That is futile and there is no need to be so hard on yourself. Making small changes can help you move forward and become more emotionally intelligent, but don't expect that you will make the smart decision or ideal response every time. While we can't manage contentment, equanimity and non-judgment like a Buddhist monk, we can still improve our experiences of our daily lives toward others and ourselves with kindness and compassion, being with 'what is', staying present and letting go of the emotional weight. The result is that we lighten up, both inside and out.

Having said all that, do your best with this practice. Keep your meditation routine going for at least 10 minutes a day and take additional mindful moments throughout your day. Refer back to the mindful experiments in these chapters from time to time and reread the concepts when you need a refresh.

Life is short and fast paced, but the practices in this book will help you slow it down and live with clearer intention and purpose. Being mindful will help you realize that everything, including life, is temporary, and sweating the small stuff is just a waste of precious time and energy.

* * *

This is just the beginning, and my hope is that I've awakened you to a new way of being. From here, continue to seek out more books, podcasts, and resources to further your journey. I've listed many of my favorites in the Resources section. My wish is that you'll discover that mindfulness is as addicting as refined sugar, but in a better, healthier and much sweeter way.

Practice the meditations in this book as often as you'd like and browse the additional bonus materials that are provided with along with the meditations. You will have access to them indefinitely, so if you didn't have time to take advantage of all of it now, they will be there when you are ready.

Download some meditation apps (also in the Resources section) and eventually you will be able to practice on your own with a timer. I always suggest guided meditations in the beginning to get going then try meditating without them in order to deepen your practice even more.

I hope that you have "savored" gaining new perspectives about yourself and others, as well as your body and the food you eat, by reading these pages. As you become more aware of and intentional with the choices you make every day—including what to put in your mouth— you will discover an increasing sense of wonder and curiosity about everything, and lots more gratitude.

As you know by now, the "Mindful Is the New Skinny" attitude is all about feeling good inside and knowing that when you do, it will be reflected beautifully on the outside. I wish you all the best on your journey and am grateful that you've allowed me to guide you on this path.

Resources

Following is a smattering of mindfulness-centered books, websites, organizations, mobile apps and other resources that have inspired me to embrace and fully live a conscious life—and can help you do the same.

Eating and Nutrition

- Institute for Integrative Nutrition, Health Coach Training Program, integrativenutrition.com
- "Am I Hungry" Mindful Eating Programs and Training, amihungry.com
- Institute for the Psychology of Eating, The World's Leading School in Nutritional Psychology, psychologyofeating.com

Holistic Centers and Studies

- The Center for Health and Healing, Mt. Kisco, NY, center4healing.net
- Westchester Buddhist Center, Irvington, NY, westchesterbuddhistcenter.org
- Omega Institute for Holistic Studies, Rhinebeck, NY, eomega.org
- New York Insight Meditation Center, New York, NY, www.nyimc.org
- Center for Mindfulness, University of Massachusetts Medical School, Shrewsbury, MA, umassmed.edu/cfm
- Kripalu Center for Yoga and Health, Stockbridge, MA, kripalu.org
- Greater Good Science Center, Science-based Insights for a Meaningful Life, University of California, Berkeley, CA, greatergood.berkeley.edu
- The Center for Mindful Living, Los Angeles, CA, mindfullivingla.org

Websites

- Hayhouse.com, publisher of inspirational and transformational books and products (I highly recommend their Hay House World Summit: hayhouseworldsummit.com)
- Mindful.org
- Everyday-mindfulness.org
- Freemindfulness.org
- UCLA Mindful Awareness Research Center, marc.ucla.edu/mindful-meditations
- Mindfulnessforteens.com
- Eileenfisherlifework.com
- Jewelneverbroken.com (singer-songwriter Jewel's movement to make happiness a habit)

Apps

- For adults: There are many mindfulness apps out there; I recommend Insight Timer, Headspace, 10%Happier, The Mindfulness App, Breathe and Calm
- For children: Mindfulness for Children
- For teens: Stop, Breathe, and Think; Smiling Mind; and Take a Break!

Books

Albers, Susan, and Lilian Cheung, *Eating Mindfully: How to End Mindless Eating and Enjoy a Balanced Relationship with Food,* New Harbinger Publications, Oakland, CA, 2012.

Brown, Brené, *Daring Greatly: How the Courage to be Vulnerable Transforms the Way we Live, Love, Parent and Lead,* Avery, New York, NY, 2015.

Chödrön, Pema, *How to Meditate: A Practical Guide to Making Friends with Your Mind,* Sounds True, Solon, OH, 2013.

Chozen Bays, Jan, *Mindful Eating: A Guide to Rediscovering a Healthy and Joyful Relationship with Food,* Shambhala (revised edition), 2017.

Harris, Dan, *10% Happier: How I Tamed the Voice in My Head, Reduced Stress Without Losing My Edge, and Found Self-Help That Actually Works: A True Story*, It Books, 2014.

Hay, Louise L., *You Can Heal Your Life,* Hay House, Carlsbad, CA, 1984.

Kabat-Zinn, Jon. *Wherever You Go, There You Are: Mindfulness Meditation in Everyday Life*, Hachette Books (10th edition), 2005.

Katie, Byron, and Stephen Mitchell, *Loving What Is: Four Questions That Can Change Your Life,* Three Rivers Press (reprint edition), 2003.

Katz, Ali, *Get the Most Out of Motherhood: A Hot Mess to Mindful Mom Parenting Guide*, Skyhorse Publishing, 2017.

Katz, Ali, *Hot Mess to Mindful Mom: 40 Ways to Find Balance and Joy in Your Everyday*, Skyhorse Publishing, 2017.

Neff, Kristin, *Self-Compassion: Stop Beating Yourself Up and Leave Insecurity Behind*, William Morrow, 2011.

Ruiz, Don Miguel, *The Four Agreements: A Practical Guide to Personal Freedom (A Toltec Wisdom Book),* Amber-Allen Publishing, San Rafael, CA, 1997.

Sincero, Jen, *You Are a Badass: How to Stop Doubting Your Greatness and Start Living an Awesome Life*, Running Press, 2013.

Stahl, Bob, and Goldstein, Elisha, *A Mindfulness-Based Stress Reduction Workbook*, New Harbinger Publications, Oakland, CA, 2010.

Tolle, Eckhart, *The Power of Now: A Guide to Spiritual Enlightenment*, Namaste Publishing, 2004

About the Author

Jodi Baretz, LCSW, CHHC is a psychotherapist and certified holistic health coach in private practice at the Center for Health and Healing in Mt. Kisco, New York. Jodi has more than two decades of experience providing clinical services and psychotherapy, as well as career and nutritional counseling.

Jodi received a Master's in Social Work from Columbia University, a Bachelor of Arts from Emory University and a certification in health coaching from the Institute for Integrative Nutrition in Manhattan. She has trained extensively in Mindfulness Based Stress Reduction (MBSR) and the integration of mindfulness and psychotherapy.

Jodi writes with authenticity about the struggles that have touched her and her clients regarding the topics of mindfulness and nutrition. Diagnosed with the autoimmune disorder Celiac Disease in her mid-thirties, Jodi experienced an awakening. She learned that there were biological answers to her health concerns, coupled with a new awareness of her body and what it could and could not tolerate. Mindfulness might have come from necessity but it opened the door to a new level of consciousness that she has incorporated into every aspect of her life.

Through Jodi's writings, her therapy practice and speaking engagements, she brings this realization to audiences in an authentic, clear and relatable manner. Jodi also contributes regularly to *Westchester Magazine*, *Inside Chappaqua* and *Armonk Magazines*, The Mindfulness App and other media outlets. She lives in Westchester with her husband and two sons and their dog Lola.

To learn more about Jodi's programs and virtual coaching through Skype:

Visit: Jodibaretz.com

Join her Facebook group: @Mindful Moms

Follow her @Mindful is the New Skinny on FB and Instagram

To invite Jodi to speak to your group:

Contact her at: jodibaretz@gmail.com

For your convenience, I have included the QR code for the Meditations and Resource Center here so you don't have to keep flipping back and forth.

http://www.mindfulisthenewskinny.com

Enjoy!

Proof

95650341R10100

Made in the USA
Columbia, SC
13 May 2018